From Award-Winning Journalist and Producer

TOM TEICHOLZ

CLOSE ENCOUNTERS
OF THE TOMMYWOOD KIND

The Sixth Installment of the **TOMMYWOOD** Series,
a Collection of Columns and Writing on Arts and Culture

A PONDWOOD PRESS BOOK

PONDWOOD PRESS
1424 4th Street, Suite 229
Santa Monica, CA 90401

Copyright © 2015 by Tom Teicholz

FIRST TRADE PAPERBACK EDITION

The majority of the articles in this collection first appeared in print in *The Jewish Journal of Los Angeles*, some in slightly different form and can also be found at tommywood.com.

All rights reserved, including the right to reproduce this book or portions thereof in any form whatsoever, including but not limited to print, audio, and electronic. For more information, address: 1424 4th Street, Suite 229, Santa Monica, CA 90401.

ISBN: 978-0-9964321-0-8

Set in Minion
Printed in the United States

For Amy and Natasha

CONTENTS

Introduction 11
The Future in Our Hands 13
Chabon's Search 19
The Bronfman Haggadah 23
Bellow by Bellow 29
Going Home with Gary Baseman 33
Son of Pacific Standard Time 45
Through the Lens of Helmut Newton 53
Q&A with Israeli Singer-Songwriter Noa 55
South African Jews Find a Home in LA 61
What Is It with Israelis and High Tech 69
Hans Richter's Future is Now! 75
Lusting For Leicas 81
Moshe Sadfie: The People's Architect 87
Remembering Rabbi Berg 93
The Long and Short of Etgar Keret 99
Lou Adler: Lucky, Low Key, and Very Cool 105
The Price of Dylan Going Electric 117
The Wallis: Now That It's Built, Will They Come? 121
Q&A with Israeli Music legend Danny Sanderson 127
We are All Inside Llewyn Davis 133
Theo Bikel Plays JewGrass 139
The Strength of Ma'aleh Film School 145
Pollock's 'Mural': Masterpiece or macho outburst? 149
Sanford 'Sandy' Frank: An Appreciation 155
Judy Fiskin: The Hammer's Summer Blockbuster 159
Jewish Heroes of The Great Patriotic War 165

Israeli Artists of the Imagination 171
The Hollywood Blacklist in Exile 177
Marx Brothers Make Merry in TV Collection 183
In Re: Artist Miri Chais' Mind 189
Leonard Cohen's Triumphant Problems 193

INTRODUCTION

This latest volume of collected columns presents a variety of *Close Encounters of the Tommywood* kind. It looks forward to high tech offerings from CES and on display at the Israel Conference and looks back at the Hollywood Blacklist in Exile. There are articles about well known writers such as Michael Chabon, Saul Bellow (though the prism of his first born son), and Etgar Keret, profiles of legends such as Lou Adler visual artists past, such as Hans Richter and Jackson Pollack and present, such as Judy Fiskin, Gary Baseman, Miri Chais, Nor Evron, and Orit Raff. There are celebrations of those long departed such as The Marx Brothers, the Jewish Heroes of the Soviet Red Army during WWII, and an appreciation of Sandy Frank, a life ended too soon. Singers and songwriters abound from Theo Bikel, to Noa and Danny Sanderson, and Los Angeles resident performer-priest, Leonard Cohen whose new album released around the time of his 80th birthday, is in itself cause for the celebration that occurs in *Tommywood*.

—Tom Teicholz
November 18, 2014

THE FUTURE IN OUR HANDS

When I was a young kid, my dad used to take me to the auto show at the old New York Coliseum, where together we looked, agog, at the cars of the future — experimental vehicles that would never see the light of day. I remember feeling bone-tired after walking the floor and being overwhelmed by all there was to see. I would clutch my dad's hand ever tighter, afraid of getting lost in the disorienting vortex of people pitching products. These memories came flooding back in early January, as I stood amid the chaos of the Consumer Electronics Show (CES) in Las Vegas.

CES, which got its start in New York City in 1967 with 250 exhibitors and 17,500 attendees, is today a four-day extravaganza with 3,000 exhibitors attracting an audience of 150,000 (as a point of comparison, that's about the entire population of Pomona) from more than 150 countries. Over the years, it's become the place where new technology is introduced, including, for example, the VCR (1970), the CD player (1981), high-definition TV (1981), 3-D TV (2009), and Ultrabooks (2012).

This was my first time at CES, held in January, and I can confirm that it is crazy-making, exhausting and frustrating. There is no way to see everything, and it's easy to miss an entire corner or row of exhibitors amid the many halls. There are also keynote speeches and panels going on throughout each day, and it would be easy to waste all of your time waiting to get in to the most popular of these. The food at the convention is pretty much what you would expect, and although you would think the organizers, after all these years, would use some of that new technology to be better prepared, the lines for buses, taxis and the monorail are reminiscent of the bread lines in the former Soviet Union. The limo drivers price-gouge, and traffic in Vegas pretty much comes to a standstill for all four days.

Yet I completely understand why so many people insist on going each year to CES: There is no better way to get a sense of the imminent future—of how we will live. I don't mean some dreamed-of George Jetson-style fantasy of jetpacks, moving sidewalks and sky-borne cars, but rather actual business trends—at CES you can see products that will be available in a matter of months on Amazon, among other places, if they are not already.

It is easy to be distracted by the hundreds (if not thousands) of businesses that didn't even exist only a few years ago, whole industries that have sprouted in response to the iPhone, iPad and other smart phones that offer every conceivable variation on cases—such as water-repellent protection coatings—or add-on devices, such as professional, HD microphones from IXY (ixymic.com), and very cool snap-on lenses from Olloolloclip.com), and portable chargers from Mophie (mophie.com), as well as some very powerful new chargers from Innergie (myinnergie.com) and in-wall adapters for speedy recharging from a reborn RCA.

There were also rows and rows of headphone companies inspired by the success of Beats, and wireless portable speakers of all shapes, sizes and brands, from the new and unknown to Marshall (marshallheadphones.com) and Monster (monstercable.com).

What got the most attention this year (and the most floor space) were the all the new "4K UltraHD TVs" (the industry name for the new TVs that pack two to four times as much information and pixels as standard 1,080P-high-definition TVs) from Samsung and Panasonic, as well as from some newcomers to the US market—HiSense and TCL—in sizes up to eighty-four inches. There was even one 110-inch HD screen. However, although these screens pack twice the info per pixel and give a remarkable level of detail, they are expensive—fifty-five-inch sets are expected to retail at around $10,000—and there is currently hardly enough 4K material available to make them must-haves.

For me, however, TVs are no longer the story.

CES made clear how much our whole notion of what a computer does is changing. Only a few short years ago, we used computers only at our desks. Now there are laptops, netbooks, the Mac Air, Ultrabooks, and tablets of all sizes. Today our iPhones or Android smart phones allow us complete portability for messaging and Internet access, and serve as media players and car navigation systems. We no longer call them computers, but "smart" devices instead.

Consumer electronics now enhance every area of human activity. Ford, Chrysler, Audi and Toyota market cars for their technology, with dashboards that look like the bridge on the starship Enterprise, including Internet-enabled sound systems.

At CES, Audi unveiled its prototype for a driverless car that can be guided by a series of radar-like sensors combined with information from the road itself (Google's prototype for such auto-piloted cars has already driven 200,000 miles across Nevada and California).

Another big theme at CES was the smart home. New ideas include being able to monitor our front-door peepholes through images relayed to our smart phones; and refrigerators, washers and dryers all becoming touch enabled, network and remote controlled (the appliances can decide at what time a cycle will run most efficiently and cost-effectively). It will soon be hard to say what isn't computerized in our home. At CES, there was even an electronic fork—an Israeli product called HAPIfork (hapilabs.com)—with warning lights that flash when you are eating too fast (or too much). Laugh if you want, but with obesity-related illnesses a major cause of death in the United States, I say: Whatever works.

Similarly, there was a whole generation of biometric devices to measure your vital signals (heart rate, pulse, blood pressure, body temperature) via wristbands, headbands and shirts, as well as activity trackers and fitness monitors from Nike (fuelband) and others such as Fitbug (fitbug.com), the latter a well-priced device (less than $50) that I was particularly impressed by. Beyond the old-fashioned pedometers, these devices help you accomplish your tasks by setting diet and exercise goals for you, suggesting ways to exceed them and rewarding you for doing so (some with firework displays, others with points redeemable for as-yet-unstated rewards).

The proliferation of such devices owes much to the newly popular psychological theory of positive feed loops. Consider, for example, those traffic signs that tell you both the speed limit and show you how fast you are going. There is no camera to catch the speeding, nor a police officer to enforce it, so no logical reason why, if you are speeding, you need to slow down. Yet the overwhelming majority of people do. In the same way, activity trackers and fitness bands suggest goals, and the brain naturally attempts to meet them. Many of these devices also provide online diary logs as well as community and support for achieving wellness goals.

For 2013, the future is not just about devices to help us be healthier, or about the devices themselves becoming smarter. They are about communication—enabling us, as much as our devices and appliances, to be in touch with one another, sharing and pushing information. Enabling us to order our food in a restaurant from a touch screen; letting our fridge send us a shopping list reminding us when we're in our car to have the car take us to a store or to a restaurant that already has our payment information on file so we just swing by and can pick up our order on our way home—a home where the security system knows us, the dishwasher and washing machine have already run at off-peak hours, and where our forks tell us to savor every bite.

It is that vision of a very real, and very near, future that makes CES so worth attending.

On the day that the simplest items in our homes become as sophisticated as the smartest device in our hands, when instead of downloading our info into our devices, technology trains us to take better care of ourselves, when our cars act as chauffeurs, we will truly have arrived at a future we cannot yet imagine. But that is already, as I write this, inevitable.

February 13, 2013

CHABON'S SEARCH

A writer walks into a room full of rabbis. This sounds like the beginning of a joke, but it's not. In the words of Woody Allen's "Broadway Danny Rose," "It's the emes." The Central Conference of American Rabbis (CCAR) held the Reform movement's annual rabbinical convention March 3-6 in Long Beach, and novelist and essayist Michael Chabon was this year's Jacob Rader Marcus lecturer. He spoke on the topic "Shaping Jewish Narrative" with Rabbi Yoel Kahn who, not co-incidentally, was the rabbi who married Chabon and his wife, author Ayelet Waldman. All of which raises the question: How is a novelist like a Reform rabbi?

Before the crowded room of gregarious, well-read rabbis from around the country, Kahn asked Chabon to narrate his own Jewish coming-of-age. When Chabon was eight, his family moved to Columbia, Md., a new planned community developed by James Rouse that sought to be a model for the city and the community of the future — fully integrated and harmonious in all aspects. It even included an interfaith spiritual center shared by several religious denominations, including Chabon's own congregation, which practiced what he called a "guitar-strumming" Reform Judaism called "Innovative Judaism."

Chabon's loss of innocence occurred at age eleven, when his parents announced their separation and eventual divorce, a completely unexpected event that caused, he said, "the scales to fall from my eyes."

Growing up, the sound of Yiddish was familiar. His grandparents belonged to a Conservative synagogue in Silver Springs, Md., which he attended on several occasions, and where they prayed, he recalled, in a "pickled-herring type of Hebrew—lots of bones in it" in a service that was heavy—not only because of its five-hour, endless-seeming plodding pace, but also because he knew there was meaning there that he couldn't yet grasp. Nevertheless after his bar mitzvah, Chabon drifted away from Judaism.

In his twenties, he said, he found himself adrift. A first marriage to a non-Jewish woman had ended. Although they'd had no children, they had fought constantly about how they would raise them. She challenged him about why he felt so strongly about his Jewish identity when he had little to no Jewish content in his life. Forced to give what Chabon called, "The Tevye answer" of "tradition," he found himself wondering what did matter to him about Judaism. And so, he said, "I began to reconnect."

Then Chabon met Waldman, and, yes, she was Jewish, but her father was a secular Trotskyist Zionist who worked on a kibbutz and had contempt for any religious practice. So, together the pair searched for what was meaningful for them, which led them, as San Francisco residents, to Rabbi Kahn's congregation.

At the same time, Chabon explained, he was also feeling equally adrift as a writer. He was publishing New Yorker-acceptable short stories, but he felt that form limited his expression of all that he enjoyed as a reader—which was all sorts of genre fiction. Chabon decided that his writing should better reflect his passions and who he was.

The Amazing Adventures of Kavalier & Clay, his Pulitzer Prize-winning novel, is about two comic book creators, one of them a Holocaust survivor; it tells the story of their lives, loves, success and tragedies, and it became, for Chabon, a vehicle for embracing his interests and expressing parts of who he was. He followed up with three more novels, *The Final Solution*, *The Yiddish Policemen's Union*, and *Gentlemen of the Road*, all of them mixing genre elements with Jewish characters and themes in new ways.

Nonetheless, Chabon said the "unapologetic Jewish stance" in his writing is only possible because he is what he called a "post-Rothian" writer, not breaking ground the way Roth or others Jewish writers of prior generations had to do.

"I benefit from the struggles of my parents and grandparents. They did all the hard work," Chabon said.

Asked how he expects his own children will connect to Judaism, Chabon said he is curious to see what they will adopt and make their own. Asked what he struggles most with as a Jew, Chabon answered that it is "the incredible black eye that fundamentalists are giving every religion," and that fundamentalists will make all religions seem tainted to his children and their generation.

In discussing how he shapes his narratives, Chabon explained that often one must decide whether to supply a lot of explanation and set things in context, or to plunge the reader right into a world and explain by means of the main character's point of view—to reveal information to the reader only as the character learns about the world.

As it turns out, the challenge for the Reform rabbi is similar, Kahn remarked, in deciding how best to explain the context of Judaism and Jewish history while attempting to address a congregant's own point of view on the world, and in so doing, shaping the narrative of Judaism for the future.

Chabon has found a way to meld his writing self with his Jewish self to forge a new narrative. And for as long as there have been American Reform rabbis, they have tried to shape the story of contemporary Judaism. As was clear from Chabon and Kahn's conversation, both the Reform rabbi and the Jewish American novelist are engaged in the search for authentic expression of self as well as a continuity of Jewish identity.

There is, however, one important distinction: Only the novelist gets to play at being God.

March 13, 2013

THE BRONFMAN HAGGADAH

For Passover this year, Rizzoli has just released *The Bronfman Haggadah*, written by the businessman, philanthropist and Jewish community leader Edgar Bronfman Sr., illustrated by artist Jan Aronson, who is also Bronfman's wife. Unlike other haggadot, this version includes the role of Moses in the story of the Exodus. In his introduction, Bronfman suggests that the omission from the traditional telling may be because the rabbis who wrote the early haggadot "viewed Moses as a dangerous hero—one who could easily upset the religious hierarchy." On the occasion of the book's release, Bronfman and Aronson talked about why and how they created the book, rethinking the role of the haggadah to tell, in their own way, the tale of Jewish Exodus and liberation. The following is an edited version of that conversation:

Tom Teicholz: Why a new haggadah?

Edgar Bronfman: What I think should be done in the 21st century [is] to have a haggadah that teaches young children what Judaism is all about. And I think it's all there in the Passover story—if you know how to tell it properly. What I've done is written a haggadah that I think children today can relate to—and not just on Passover.

TT: How is this haggadah different from all other haggadot?

EB: It's different in a number of ways. First, and this was my wife's idea: Why do you want to feed Elijah after you've finished your meal? If Elijah represents the poor of the world, then surely you should let him in to share the meal with you. Young people will learn that feeding the poor—that's very Jewish. The second thing that's different, very much different, is I don't talk about the four children; I talk about the four different kinds of Jews there are in this world and how we have to have open arms to all of them to bring them back into our fold. The third thing that's different, I don't stop at the Red Sea and I don't call it the Red Sea. I call it the Sea of Reeds—a shallow part of the Red Sea that the Jews crossed without thinking, but that when the Egyptians with their chariots and their armor came, they sunk. That put the Jews on the other side of the Red Sea. No one's chasing them now. And they're free. Free to do anything and everything, and that becomes chaos. So Moses leads them to Mount Sinai and gives them the Ten Commandments, and this the Jews accept because they can't stand the chaos either. And that's where I end [the narrative], rather than at the Red Sea.

TT: You mention the four types of Jews (the wise, rebellious, simple and indifferent). Who do you see as the audience for this haggadah?

EB: I see the audience for this haggadah as the young people who have not left Judaism but are not affiliated. ... Hopefully this revives some interest—just like a Birthright trip to Israel revives interest in Judaism.

TT: Throughout your life, you've set yourself the task of very large projects, whether it's running Seagram's or leading the World Jewish Congress or addressing the third phase of life. Why did you, at this point in your life, decide to tackle one holiday, one night, one meal?

EB: I think Passover is the most important of the Jewish holidays…[It's] the night we became a people…I think all the elements of Judaism are encapsulated in this story…[Also], when children come to the table at Passover, they are happy… that's a good time to teach them a little Judaism.

TT: Ms. Aronson, tell me a little about your artistic journey with this project.

Jan Aronson: With this particular project a couple of things happened that were unique in my career. Number one, I was able to do a lot of research into how I wanted the imagery to cohere with the history of certain aspects of the haggadah. [For example,] I thought it would be interesting to put in a biblical map, which is not something I've ever seen in a haggadah…I added the map [to] put some interesting context and historical references that we are talking about in a visual form…

My work is very painterly…This gave me an opportunity to branch out and do other things with my work that I'd never had the opportunity to do. I was also able to draw on some of the skills that I had but hadn't used in a long time. It was a chance to play and have a good time with patterns and imagery and go outside the box with certain illustrations.

TT: Did working on these illustrations give you any deeper insight into the haggadah?

JA: I thought a lot about which concepts I wanted to illustrate. The ones that were very important to me [from] a spiritual, metaphysical and also ethical standpoint were the ones I was drawn to. [For example,] the burning bush in my concept... [occurs at] sunrise while [Moses] is meditating on his life...The sun is rising and the color is coming through the shrubbery of the desert. He decides to go back and deal with what he left in Egypt as well as meet his brother, whom he had never met...

TT: On a lighter note, this haggadah does not make the seder shorter.

EB: My idea was not to make it short. My idea was to make it so that when you were finished with it, you had really done the seder and you had squeezed out a lot of knowledge of Judaism from it.

TT: You left songs for the end rather than integrate them in the seder. Any reason for that?

EB: I think singing is fun, but the [songs] don't have much to say much Jewishly...Well, at the end you've had your fourth glass of wine, you're kind of relaxed. It's fun to sing. If the children have gone to bed by then, we don't care. What I care about is what we can teach them up until the time of the dinner.

TT: You introduce quotes from Frederick Douglass, [Ralph Waldo] Emerson and Marge Piercy as part of your seder.

EB: My rabbis.

TT: Your rabbis. To that point, this struck me as a secularist haggadah. The magic of faith doesn't seem to play as great a role.

EB: The magic tricks and all that are good storytelling. I'm not sure it all happened, and I don't think it teaches very much.

TT: As I read it, there is one omission in your haggadah, and please correct me if I missed it. We are commanded at the seder to feel as if we were slaves in Egypt. For me, the great contribution of Judaism to the world is first, monotheism and the notion of a living God that is not embodied in literal idols and is an abstract concept; and second, this commandment at the seder that speaks to empathy, one of the greatest features of the Jewish faith. But you don't mention this commandment.

EB: [As to the contributions of Judaism to the world] I say a little more [about this] at the end, where the [Israelites] are all fighting and killing each other. It's chaotic. Then Moses gives them the Ten Commandments. By accepting the Ten Commandments, they become God's people. I want to leave it at that…because it's impossible for most people to really imagine themselves as "this is the night we were freed from Egypt." That's a stretch. Nice words, but it doesn't mean very much.

TT: Each of you has worked for many years in your separate spheres. Can you talk about working together?

EB: For me, that was a joy. What I did was I asked my wife if she would illustrate the haggadah. She said, "But I'm not an illustrator." I said, "I want someone who's fresh, and not encumbered." I know my wife is bright and smart, and I know what a great artist she is [and that with her participation], I'm going to go from what I know is a good haggadah to a great one, by having it become beautiful.

JA: I had the opportunity of a lifetime. Number one, to collaborate with my husband, whom I adore and I respect, on a project that he already had worked five years to perfect…and he said, "Here, just take it and fly with it"—it was a tremendous opportunity and a lot, a lot of fun. I had total freedom, and when I would go into Edgar's office and show him one of the paintings I had done…He was always really happy with it. So it was a wonderful collaboration in a very special way.

TT: On that note, let me say: Hag Sameach.
EB & JA: Hag Sameach to you, too.
March 22, 2013

BELLOW BY BELLOW

Sons of famous fathers rarely eclipse their parent. Although there are some notable exceptions (JFK and Justice Oliver Wendell Holmes come to mind), the singularity of purpose, the ruthlessness that lead to lasting renown, as well as the perks and vicissitudes that come with fame, none of these reward excellent parenting nor allow children the same crucible to ignite a flame that might burn brighter than their parent's. That children of the famous write memoirs is common; that they have insight is less so.

This comes to mind because on April 25, Writers Bloc presents Saul Bellow & The Holocaust: Gregory Bellow With Rabbi David Wolpe, on the occasion of the publication of *Saul Bellow's Heart: A Son's Memoir* (Bloomsbury). The event will take place at Temple Emanuel of Beverly Hills.

Gregory Bellow (or Greg, as I'll refer to him), lives in Redwood City, Calif., and has been a practicing therapist for some forty years. In a recent phone conversation, he described himself as a "contemporary psychoanalytic therapist" who was much influenced by the work of psychoanalyst Heinz Kohut, who developed self-psychology. As he explained: "Most theories of the self seem to have two components: a more inner-directed and a more outer-directed self."

His approach in writing his memoir was much the same: to reveal the inner Bellow, the one the public never saw, and contrast him with the public figure. "I was definitely attempting to write a narrative that was emanating from the inside out," Greg said. "I try to understand myself and my father and our relationship as deeply as I could."

The public Saul Bellow accomplished great things: Following his first two novels, *Dangling Man* and *The Victim*, Bellow burst forth with *The Adventures of Augie March*, which took the 19th century bildungsroman and rendered it in 20th century vernacular, its prose dancing to a Yiddish nigun in a distinctly American way. Before *Augie*, American Jews writing fiction were not considered worthy; Bellow opened the doors. Back then, Greg recalled, "Jews did not belong in the literary firmament. Saul and his brilliant friends proved them wrong."

Bellow continued to produce vexing, challenging and wildly pleasurable novels throughout his long career; even his late novellas, such as *More Die of Heartbreak* and *Ravelstein*, had their pleasures.

But Saul Bellow, the man, was a more complex matter. Born into a Yiddish-speaking home and able at an early age to recite long passages from the Torah in Hebrew, he escaped getting his hands dirty, literally, in the family coal business, by writing. In his twenties and thirties, he was imbued with leftist politics (he actually paid his respects to Leon Trotsky's body in a Mexican morgue) and distanced himself from Jewish observance and identity. He spent the 1940s so completely focused on his writing and his self that he paid little attention to the fate of the Jews in Europe, for which he expressed great guilt later in life.

However, after Israel's Six-Day War, which he witnessed as a correspondent, Bellow reaffirmed his Jewish identity. In the years that followed, as the American far left abandoned Israel, Bellow became increasingly neoconservative in keeping with his fellow University of Chicago faculty, which included Milton Friedman and Allan Bloom.

"Going to see Israel and witnessing the war firsthand was absolutely pivotal," Greg said, "When I speak in LA, I'm going to embellish on that. I'm going to advance a hypothesis about what was going on or what may have been going on." He promised "a literary psychological hypothesis that I'm going to keep in suspense until the event."

Saul Bellow's private life was equally complicated. He married five times, had numerous affairs, bore four children — each from a different wife (the youngest born when Saul was eighty-four). Greg gives portraits of all of the women in his father's life, but the pain his mother endured still reads fresh.

"Everything was secondary to writing in my father's life," Greg said. "And that was the way it was."

In 1976, Saul Bellow was awarded the Nobel Prize in Literature, the first American to win since John Steinbeck in 1962, and the first -Jewish-American to receive the honor. After that, in Greg's telling, his father was "thought of more by what he wrote than who he was."

Nonetheless, at his father's funeral in 2005, Greg was struck by all those who knew Bellow as a literary figure, but saw themselves as his son. The title of his memoir's introductory chapter, "Awakened by a Grave Robbery," explains how that made him feel. At a panel later that year, Greg spoke about his father and began to feel he had something to say. He was further encouraged by a "long heart-to-heart conversation" with Janna Malamud Smith, Bernard Malamud's daughter, also a psychotherapist, who wrote a perceptive and well-received memoir of her father (*My Father Is a Book*) that, Greg said, "was pivotal in my decision."

He said he wanted people to understand something "about my father's complexity, his humanness," adding, "and I don't think anyone else is in a position to make that case but me because I knew him so long, and I knew him so intimately, and I knew him in the way that I knew him."

Although the book reveals things that Greg is sure his father would not have wanted made public, Greg felt it was his turn to speak about the man so many others claimed as their own.

"My father was a very complicated man," Greg concluded. "He was definitely difficult to live with at times. I make that very clear in the book. I make it very clear that it took a toll on me, but I don't think I'm doing him any harm." When he finished the memoir, Greg' gave it to his wife to read. Her review: "The love comes through on every page."

This love, however, in true Bellow fashion, is a most complex affair.

April 18, 2013

GOING HOME WITH GARY BASEMAN

There's an old saying that goes something like this: We spend the first half of our lives running away from home and the rest trying to get back. Consider Homer, way back in ancient Greece, who defined our notion of a life's odyssey as a journey that begins and ends at home.

The same could be said of Gary Baseman, a Los Angeles artist whose career retrospective opens this weekend at the Skirball Cultural Center. Baseman organized the show thematically, inspired by the rooms of his childhood home—Living Room (Welcome), Dining Room (Celebration), Hallway (Journey), Kitchen (Feast), Bedroom (The Human Condition). All of the artworks are installed alongside actual furniture and artifacts from the house where he grew up, along with some objects from his relatives' homes. Personal history is an ongoing inspiration for Baseman: He's currently working on a new series titled "Journey to My Mythical Homeland."

Baseman is a highly eclectic artist whose very personal iconography recalls such diverse traditions as Rudolph Dirks'

Sunday comic strips "The Katzenjammer Kids"; the underground artist R. Crumb and Raw comics; the haunting psychic landscapes of Picabia and Dali; and the multimedia and multiplatform work of such post-Warholian Pop artists as Keith Haring, Kenny Scharf and Takashi Murakami. Baseman does it all—paintings, prints, advertising, commercial illustration, TV series, animated film, toys, wallets, stickers, installations, and performances—the sum total of which Baseman calls his "pervasive practice."

His distinctive style has been consistent since childhood; it features anthropomorphized animals and invented creatures, as well as women and children, all of which are depicted in toy- or doll-like form or transformed into mythical creatures. Many of the images are shown traveling through crowded, dream-like landscapes. At the same time, the creatures and narratives of Baseman's paintings and various series coincide metaphorically with the artist's maturation as an artist and with the events of his personal life.

Baseman's work has been exhibited in museums and galleries all over the world, however Los Angeles is his home, and at the Skirball he really wants to bring his audience into his world, to inspire each visitor to feel at home with all his artistic creations.

When I visited him recently at his Los Angeles studio and current home, Baseman welcomed me with Old World manners into his repository of obsessions and collections—a deluge of toys, photos and advertising artifacts from the 1930s and '40s worthy of the Collyer brothers as well as a treasure trove of his art in various stages of completion. We talked for two-and-a-half hours, and the conversation easily could have lasted many hours more.

Baseman's parents met in a displaced persons camp after World War II; both are originally from towns in what was then Poland (now Ukraine) outside of Rovno (Rivne). His father, Ben, escaped from his town, Berezne, into the nearby forests, and fought with a Russian partisan unit; Baseman's mother, Naomi, survived because her city, Kostopol, fell under Soviet domination.

The artist was born in 1960 in Los Angeles; he's a full decade younger than his siblings and the only native U.S. citizen in the family (his brother Morris was born in Austria, brother Sam and sister Netta in Canada). Baseman was, he said, his parents' "American Dream" baby—the one who could grow up to become president. Although his parents and most of their friends were Holocaust survivors, they didn't want to burden him with their past. Yet as he was told on childhood trips to Israel—one at age four with his mother, the other at twelve with his father—the reason his parents had survived so much, the reason they worked so hard and even the reason Israel was founded, was all for him.

He was the hope of the next generation. No pressure. All he had to do was excel and succeed.

His parents spoke English with thick accents and spoke Yiddish to one another and to other Holocaust survivors, a language as foreign yet as familiar to Baseman as the Spanish that surrounded him in the rest of his city. His father, an electrician, did not talk much, but when he did, it was of survival and sacrifice, and he inculcated Baseman with the mantra that if you work hard and are a good person, anything is possible. If there ever were a problem, he would say in his Yiddish-accented English, "The door is always open." Those words became the title of the Skirball exhibition.

Baseman's mother worked at the bakery counter of Canter's Deli on Fairfax for more than forty years, at a time when Canter's was very much the epicenter of Fairfax's Jewish district. The family lived in one unit of a four-plex on Curson Avenue, a half block from the old Pan Pacific Auditorium, the Streamline Moderne architectural gem that closed in 1972 and burned down in 1989, but which Baseman cites as having influenced his early aesthetic. When Baseman was five, the family moved to another apartment a few blocks away, on Detroit Street.

Given that his parents worked long hours, Baseman was a latchkey kid, left mostly to his own devices. He attended area public schools: Third Street Elementary, John Burroughs Middle School—his bar mitzvah was at the Orthodox Shaarei Tefila on Beverly Boulevard—and Fairfax High School. Although he has never had any formal art training, Baseman knew early on that he wanted to be an artist. At eleven, he twice won the monthly Bob's Big Boy art contest, and in 1978 he won the Area E art contest judged by Sergio Aragones of Mad magazine and Stan Lee of Marvel Comics. From Fairfax High, he won the Distinguished Art Service award for illustrating the school newspaper and the yearbook.

He went on to UCLA, graduating from there as a communications major, magna cum laude and Phi Beta Kappa. He says he was driven to be the "goodest" student, with perfect attendance, great grades—and the most moral, never breaking any rules, even to jaywalk or have a drink before his 21st birthday.

After graduation, Baseman felt the responsible thing to do was to pursue a commercial art career while continuing to make art, "on the side." He did a short stint at an ad agency, but that did not really agree with him, so he began to pursue work as a commercial illustrator. An image he made for the cover of *The New York Times Sunday Book Review* put him on the map.

To make his American Dream come true, Baseman moved to New York in 1986. "The advertising and publishing and art world were all in New York," he said. At the time, he believed, "Every major artist was in New York, and if you lived in LA you were a substandard regional artist. You had to go there."

He became a successful commercial illustrator: "I did twelve to twenty assignments every month for ten years," Baseman said. "I didn't take a lot of vacations; I was really there to work." *The New York Times* assignment was followed by *TIME*, *Rolling Stone*, *The New Yorker*, and *Entertainment Weekly*. He also created commercial campaigns for Gatorade, Nike, and Mercedes-Benz. Baseman won several illustration awards, including the prestigious Art Directors Club award. He was also realizing his own Ralph Lauren-esque transformation, marrying Mary Ellen Williges, a beautiful and stylish All-American girl, and settling in the suburbs.

At the same time, commercial work was increasingly being seen as art, while underground comics and graphic novels were going mainstream. Photographer Robert Mapplethorpe did commercial work, director Tim Burton was making live-action and animated feature films, cartoonist Art Spiegelman won a Pulitzer for "Maus," and Spiegelman's wife, Francoise Mouly, the former editor of Raw, became cartoon editor at The New Yorker. The outlaws were becoming the insiders. Illustrators such as William Joyce were doing Disney children shows, and Klasky Csupo's "Rugrats" ruled Nickelodeon.

Baseman, whose art design is featured on the popular board game Cranium, saw the opportunity and began to pitch TV concepts. He made two pilots for Nickelodeon that never aired, however the experience gave him "the hunger to get a show on the air," as well as the realization that for TV, "I need to be in LA." Which was just as well. Baseman found New York's weather too severe and life there too harsh—there were some things he could not get over, such as "the smell of urine in the Broadway-Lafayette subway station."

Los Angeles was more to his liking. He sold a show, *Teacher's Pet*, which began airing on the Disney Channel in 2000 and became a great success, winning four Emmys, including an outstanding performer win for Nathan Lane. Baseman enjoyed the collaboration with other animation artists and with writers Bill and Cherie Steinkellner, as well as making the *Teacher's Pet* movie in 2004. At the same time, Baseman was invited to show his art in a serious gallery, the Peter Mendenhall Gallery in Pasadena and to work with Kidrobot to create limited-edition designer toys. Baseman purchased a beautiful home for his wife and himself in Hancock Park.

The American Dream, indeed.

Yet Baseman's work from this period, from 2000 to 2005, tells a different story. His creatures and landscapes of this period seem unresolved—childlike yet adult, infantile yet serious, at play and yet in danger. His images of females are idealized, asexual objects of veneration. It is an unreal world of arrested teenage development where everything appears OK—in turmoil but devoid of conflict, and where sex does not exist and desire is frightening and held in abeyance.

"I hid in my work," Baseman said, explaining that there was "a sense of desire and longing and lust in my work, and I felt it was oozing out of me, in my pores, and in my characters…

[such as] these 'infinity girls,' whose arms and legs entwine like the infinity sign but they are just out of reach. You can't obtain them." Baseman's state of mind at that time is perhaps best revealed by his character The Happy Idiot, which, Baseman explains, is "the snowman who's willing to sacrifice himself for the mermaid, melt himself down so she can live."

In 2005, Baseman started painting forests and created a narrative about "running into the woods and this creature licking my wounds and bringing me back to life and then devouring me." He didn't make the connection at the time, but today he has come to recognize that the forest evokes the place into which his father escaped to survive the war.

Baseman had also created a series of piñata paintings beginning in 2002 in which the characters' guts are laid bare, literally. These could be seen as showing how Baseman was being torn apart by his inner turmoil. Increasingly, his paintings told the story of a struggle between creatures of what he called "Creamy Goodness" and creatures of desire.

In 2005, Baseman introduced his now-signature character, Toby, who looks a bit like a Bizarro fez-wearing Mickey Mouse and whom Baseman claims is his alter ego. Toby began to appear in travel photos—at the Sistine Chapel, with Michelangelo, looking like he is holding up the Leaning Tower of Pisa. Baseman calls Toby "the keeper of the secrets." Which begs the question, if Baseman was so "good," what secrets did he have to hide?

Raised to be good and to always see good in the world, Baseman nevertheless had a clear view of hypocrisy, the unhappy lives of suburban America, the corruption of politicians and the deceit of evangelists. Even the Orthodox Jews his father held up as pious were often revealed in the media as having feet of clay. Baseman had come to realize that no one really cared that he had never skipped class in high school, and he found that whatever success he had achieved did not keep him from unhappiness; that suppressing his secret desires, longings and dreams or painting them did not make them go away.

Even harder for him to admit was that maybe these yearnings were good, not bad. Maybe the world wasn't as his father raised him to view it. Baseman had a hard time admitting all this—or that he was unhappy in his marriage.

In a life where he succeeded at everything he worked at, Baseman couldn't countenance a failed marriage. Even after separating from his wife in 2006, he couldn't admit as much to his parents, who only learned of the impending divorce from his wife.

Baseman moved out of his Hancock Park home and into the ground-floor apartment of a Carthay Circle duplex. He continued to avoid confronting his reality by traveling and enjoying being newly single. He was, he now says, literally running away from himself. In his paintings from this era, about 2006 to 2009, his characters are shown traveling through a forest, sometimes carrying rifles. Into this environment appear the new characters, Wild Girls, who hold the promise of joy in the moment, without deeper commitment. They, in turn, are beset by little demons suggesting that pleasure is not without its danger.

In 2009, Baseman returned to Israel for the first time in thirty-six years to teach at the Bezalel Art Academy. While in Israel, Baseman also had a show of his work, which he called "The Sacrifice of Ooga"—ooga(sponge cake) being Baseman's favorite Hebrew word as a child. His canvases were filled with his Wild Girls, who represented Baseman's own sexual revolution, and other characters called "Chouchous," who represented the still unattainable bliss and goodness that was complicated by all his demons. In contrast to these creatures representing Baseman's id, he also created a dragon, his super-ego, a symbol for those parental demands that kept him even from jaywalking.

Baseman knew what had to happen: "I had to sacrifice that dragon, to kill it." But he was surprised by what he did: "When I got there, I couldn't slay it." Baseman said, adding: "I tried in my art, but I'm still working on it [in my personal life]."

I suggested to Baseman that perhaps he could not slay the dragon and free himself of the inhibitions caused by his parents' expectations because he discovered the dragon was not a creature apart from him—it was a part of him. To wit: In Israel, Baseman found he had come to the end of his running away. Baseman needed to make peace with his past and with himself. The journey, wherever it took him, was now as much inner- as it was outward-directed. It was time to return home.

Although Baseman had confronted the burden of his parents' dreams, he nonetheless had to face their mortality. In 2010, his father, who'd always had a tremendous will to live, even recovering and thriving after diabetes-related leg amputations, died at the age of ninety-three.

"When my father passed…I realized that I was the keeper of his story, and if I didn't tell his story, it would be lost forever." While visiting with some distant cousins in Israel, Baseman learned of the existence of ayizkor (memorial) book from his father's town that his father had never told him, or any of Baseman's siblings, about. Baseman wondered why. After his father's death, he found the book hidden in a container in a closet filled with bills and other papers. The book contained several pages describing his father's heroism as a partisan.

Baseman realized how little he knew about where his parents had come from. "To know those stories, I needed to go there and pay my respects."

So, last year, Baseman received a Fulbright fellowship to teach at the Art Academy in Riga, Latvia. From there, through social media, he connected with two artist friends who lived in Lviv, Ukraine—Jana Brike and Aigars Bikse—who arranged for him to come to Lviv to speak to art students from all over Ukraine. They also offered to drive with him from Riga to Lviv, and then on to his parents' towns, outside Rivne.

"It was very emotional…To travel through Warsaw and Lodz, going through Krakow and Auschwitz and going though Lviv and heading through Rovno, and even doing interviews on Ukraine National TV and Lviv local TV, telling my story and also visiting my parents' towns," he said.

Today, he said, his parents' hometowns are very suburban, and there are few traces of the former Jewish life there. Baseman was able to find where his mother's home once stood, and he walked along the path where her relatives were taken to be murdered and left in a mass grave. In his father's town, he found the abandoned cemetery where his great-grandfather was buried, but the gravestones had all been taken for use in another building. There was a memorial at the mass grave of his paternal grandparents, and he paid his respects there.

As a personal art project, Baseman had his friends from Lviv print photos of his grandfather and frame them. They nailed them to trees in the cemetery where his grave should be.

Baseman put on a costume he had made, of a giant magi with a cone-like head with one giant all-seeing eye, and wearing an apron with the Hebrew word for truth, emet, printed across his chest (emet is also the word that activates the golem). Baseman's friends photographed him wearing the costume, not only in the cemeteries but also in his parents' towns. "To let people know there and everywhere that you can't hide the truth," he said, and to remind them "that [there are] souls there."

Which brings us back to the exhibition, organized by Skirball curators Doris Berger, Erin Clancey and Erin Curtis.

During his emotional trip to Eastern Europe, Baseman thought: "I'm going crazy, and this is what my parents were protecting me from. I opened up Pandora's Box." However, when he got home, he decided, "If anyone's going to make sense of it, I'm going to." So he told the Skirball: "I know what I want to do...I want to bring my home into the place...because every room represents a theme in my work."

Last October, as Baseman was preparing for the show, going though all his archives and material, his mother died. She was in her early 90s. And Baseman said he misses her greatly, especially her cooking—particularly the homemade gefilte fish she served on holidays.

"Both my mom and dad were able to die in their home, at peace, with their family around," he said. "With all they went through, and to show their kids that there's nothing to be afraid from death...except, well, that I'm next, which did kind of freak me out."

Baseman recognizes the irony that "I'm creating a show called 'The Door Is Always Open' and this is the first time that my parents' actual door is not going to be open, because it's gone." As for the rest of us, however, we will all be able to visit Baseman's home at the Skirball and see that, although he may still feel himself to be a work in progress, Baseman is finally at home in the world.

April 24, 2013

SON OF PACIFIC STANDARD

I t's back!
Remember long ago in those dark days of 2011, when "Pacific Standard Time," the Getty-sponsored initiative, got more than sixty cultural organizations throughout Southern California to shine a light on the impact of Los Angeles' art scene between 1945 and 1980? Well, given the success of that first effort, the Getty has now launched "Son of PST" (my name) or, as the Getty calls it, "Pacific Standard Time Presents," a smaller-scale initiative of 11 affiliated shows about "modern architecture in LA" (visit pacificstandardtimepresents.org for complete details).

For its part, the J. Paul Getty Museum is offering "Overdrive: LA Constructs the Future 1940-1990" at the Getty Center through July 21. In truth, Wim de Wit, head of the Department of Architecture and Contemporary Art at the Getty Research Institute, along with curator Christopher Alexander, had been working for several years on this show, but the Getty saw an opportunity to launch the exhibition as part of a larger network of related shows and, in conjunction, to feature programming on the subject at institutions throughout Los Angeles.

Organized thematically, "Overdrive" features photographs, architectural drawings and models, films, digital displays and contemporary art, all organized around several themes, such as car culture (diners, drive-ins, auto design), urban networks (freeways, water and power buildings), engines of innovation (oil, aviation, aerospace industry buildings), higher education (UCLA, Art Center College of Design in Pasadena and UC Riverside among others), international commerce (LAX); and media and entertainment industries (studios and theme parks); community magnets (faith, culture, sports, shopping); and residential architecture (including designs and models for the Santa Monica homes of now-superstar architects Frank Gehry and Thom Mayne).

The concept may sound a little all over the place, but in truth the show is mostly about buildings, the dreams that inspired them, the plans their builders had for them, what got built as well as what didn't, and the influences those buildings wrought—all meant, in the words of the exhibition's introduction, to "highlight some of the region's most ambitious urban experiments."

Fitting for a show organized by the Research Institute, a library, "Overdrive," is more conceptual and research-driven than a conventional image-centered museum exhibition. As such, it is part of a trend among some art museums to extend the scope of what's shown in their galleries to include popular, historical, social and cultural artifacts. This has been the province of the Museum of Modern Art in New York since its founding in 1929, but otherwise was much more the province of non-art, history and humanities museums, such as the Grammy Museum or even the Autry National Center, but as Bob Dylan put it so long ago, "The times they are a-changin."

"With an architecture show, it's really difficult to tell a story, and to tell a story in a visually compelling manner," the Getty's Rani Singh, one of the show's co-curators, told me. "For us, the challenge was really to tell a very complicated story of the city of Los Angeles and how it developed," she said. "To do that in a visually compelling and strong way was a real challenge."

There are nuggets of information to be mined throughout the exhibit. For example, did you know that the Googie-style architecture of the Norm's coffee shops was designed to recall an automobile showroom? Or that LAX called itself "the first airport of the Jet Age"? That the Capitol Records building, the world's first circular building, put its recording studios in the basement for better sound-proofing and features built-in sun shades for its windows; or that the needle on its tower used to broadcast "Hollywood" in Morse code—and a relative of Samuel Morse was the first person to broadcast that message from its antenna? That the pools of water outside the Department of Water and Power building are recirculated to cool the building, and that originally that building, designed by A. C. Martin and Associates, was meant to be illuminated twenty-four hours a day? The exhibition abounds with such fascinating minutiae.

The original drawings for Universal City are included, as well showing how it truly was intended to be citylike, including multifamily residential apartments mixed with hotels surrounding an entertainment street. There are even photos of Howard Hughes' Spruce Goose, shown both out in the water and in its hangar. And images of the four-level interchange of freeways—under construction and completed—highlight their importance and strange architectural beauty (something now lost on most of us as we curse the traffic). In the section on community engagement, photos show Dodger Stadium being built, as well as the forcible evictions in the former site of Chavez Ravine.

Great film clips are embedded throughout the exhibit, such as one of Edward R. Murrow taking viewers on a tour of CBS' Television City. In a case of saving the best for last, at the tail end of the exhibit, one can sit down and watch a selection of "oral histories"—produced interviews. These include the late Julius Schulman talking about the growth of Los Angeles, complete with all his much-missed boosterish egocentrism, and Frank Gehry explaining how being part of L.A.'s art scene with Wallace Berman, among others, forever influenced his work, and how his childhood study of Talmud sparked his disputatious spirit. David C. Martin talks of three generations of architects in Los Angeles, and in one interview, structural engineer Richard Bradshaw, talking about the construction of LAX, explains that an architect is, literally, as the title implies, the arch technician of a building project, an etymology I had never before considered.

What the Getty exhibition makes clear is that the Los Angeles urban landscape we now take for granted was built building by building. Photos of the Music Center under construction (including the famous Schulman image of the Mark Taper Forum), UCLA's construction boom in the 1960s, and the impact of Disneyland on popular culture and theme parks all are here. The show also highlights how houses of worships in Los Angeles, such as the Sidney Eisenshtat-designed Sinai Temple, used, according to the catalog, "sculptural designs and bold forms to impact the streetscape." And how the harmonious design of the First A.M.E. Church in

Los Angeles matched the calming effect the church sought for its parishioners in the wake of the Rodney King verdict.

The Getty exhibition hopes to make us really see Los Angeles. "This is a city we all inhabit, we all drive though, we walk though, we live and breathe and eat in this city," Singh said. "And these buildings become intimate in a way, and hopefully with our exhibition, one comes out with a different understanding and an appreciation for the city that we live in and the level of beauty here."

May 15, 2013

THROUGH THE LENS OF HELMUT NEWTON

Many years ago, on Jan. 23, 2004, to be precise, I was driving west on Sunset Boulevard when traffic stopped completely. There were police and an ambulance in front of the Chateau Marmont, where a car had crashed. I figured some celebrity-laden party had gotten out of hand, but later that night I learned that photographer Helmut Newton, the "King of Kink," so-called for his shots of modern Valkyries posed like extras from Cavani's "The Night Porter" or Sally Bowles' co-workers at the Cabaret, had died, crashing his Cadillac into a wall across the street from the Chateau, the 83-year-old artist's Los Angeles home base.

A retrospective of Newton's work opens June 29 at the Annenberg Space for Photography, including his giant nudes, some featured in eight-by-eight-foot prints made specifically for the exhibition. As Wallis Annenberg, CEO, president and chairman of the board of the Annenberg Foundation said in a statement accompanying the exhibition: "Helmut Newton is one of the most powerful and influential photographers of the past century—the place where art and fashion and subversion and aspiration all collide."

He was also one of a handful of photographers who transformed fashion photography, and fashion advertising, into artworks, greater than the products they were selling (Irving Penn and Richard Avedon also come to mind). But even among this notable group, Newton's work stood apart — both easily identifiable and much-imitated for the way he cast his models, often tall, blond and frequently naked, as either out-of-reach goddesses or playthings to be dominated and fetishized. Newton had a way of making both his subjects and his viewers complicit in the images' sexual innuendo, or as Annenberg put it: "If Newton's work was controversial, I believe it's because he expressed the contradictions within all of us, and particularly within the women he photographed so beautifully: empowerment mixed with vulnerability, sensuality tempered by depravity."

Given the exploration of power and debauchery within his work, it may come as little surprise to discover that Newton was born Helmut Neustadter in Berlin in 1920 to a prosperous Jewish family; his father owned a button factory. At twelve, Newton purchased his first camera, and by 16 he was an apprentice to Yva (Elise Simon), a photographer who specialized in covering the German theater. If one is to believe Newton's 2003 autobiography, "Helmut Newton" (Random House), the Nazis' rise to power and the passage of the anti-Semitic Nuremberg Laws were merely an inconvenience to him, as Yva could no longer work (she would later be deported and murdered at Auschwitz), and because the beautiful blond girl he had a crush on rejected him. For his part, Newton went on to spend the rest of his life both idealizing Aryan blondes and making them submit to his will.

In 1938, following Kristallnacht, Newton's father was briefly imprisoned in a concentration camp, forced to abandon the factory and flee with Newton's mother to South America. Newton, then eighteen, could not get a visa and was sent instead to China. He made it as far as Singapore, where, according to his autobiography, he became a gigolo, or, at least the kept boyfriend of a much-older divorcee. From Singapore, he made his way to Australia in 1942, where he was interned by the British as a German national. Released to serve in the Australian army, at war's end in 1945, he took Australian citizenship and changed his name to Newton.

After the war, Newton started a photo portraiture business in Melbourne where he met the actress June Brown, who would become his wife and partner. Newton spent the 1950s shooting for Australian and then British Vogue. In the 1960s, he moved to Paris to work for French Vogue. By the seventies, his work was being featured in Vogue and Harper's Bazaar, as well as for Yves Saint Laurent.

Yet no matter where he was, Newton brought a 1920s Berlin sensibility to his work. His images, always in black and white, explored fetishes not seen in polite culture—such as scantily clad models in leg casts or wearing orthopedic braces; or in leather corsets, with whips. In the Annenberg show, photos from this era show women dressed as men, women kissing women, women on all fours wearing a saddle, women in garters, in high heels and stilettos and not much else—images meant to provoke, to incite and, most important, to hold one's attention, as if giving us a peephole view into an unfolding narrative.

In addition to the more than one hundred prints featured in the show, the Annenberg will also screen two films about the artist, both showing continuously in the galleries: "Helmut by June," was directed by June Newton, wife of fifty-six years (also a professional photographer, working under the name Alice Springs), and in the film she goes behind the scenes at photo shoots and in their homes to discuss his work and their private life over the years. Also showing will be an original documentary commissioned by the Annenberg from Arclight Productions, including interviews with Newton's models, stylists and fashion editors, as well as his assistants and friends.

After Newton's death, fellow German fashion icon Karl Lagerfeld told *The New York Times*: "Berlin was him, he was Berlin…He was a graphic artist with a sense of composition in his imagery, with Berlin's silent movies and a whole history in his pictures…He was the last artist who had that Jewish wit, the last link to a Germany that I did not know but that I can understand." A Germany that was murdered out of existence, that Newton really didn't know either—not the Jewish part—and whose decadence he could only observe, as a young apprentice, staring through a lens, wanting in.

May 29, 2013

Q&A WITH ISRAELI SINGER-SONGWRITER NOA

Achinoam Nini, the Israeli singer-songwriter known to all simply as Noa, will perform on June 18 at American Jewish University as part of the new Geller Festival of the Arts. Born in Tel Aviv in 1969, Noa moved to New York as a child and lived there with her family until she returned to Israel at 16. After her military service as part of an entertainment unit, Noa went on to Israel's Rimon music school, where she met Gil Dor, now her longtime songwriting partner and musical accomplice; the twenty-three-year collaborators will perform together in Los Angeles. Based in Israel, but a truly international artist, she performs in English, French, Italian, Spanish, Thai, Hindi, Arabic, Hebrew and the language of the Yemenite Jews, the last being her own heritage. Noa is also an outspoken peace activist and has performed (and spoken) at the Davos World Economic Forum, sung for Pope John Paul II, performed at LIVE 8 and was in the finals of the 2009 Eurovision contest performing with Israeli-Arab singer Mira Awad. She spoke by phone from her home in Israel, and the following is an edited version of the conversation:

Tom Teicholz: Will you be doing material from your most recent album, "The Israeli Songbook," in your performance here?

Noa: First, a little background: I am a singer-songwriter, and most of my career has been based on original material in English and Hebrew. I grew up in the United States, so English is my first language. I write mostly in English, but I also write music to Hebrew poetry...[However], two years ago, I did an album that pays homage to classic Hebrew songs that I called "The Israeli Songbook."

TT: How would you describe these songs?

Noa: They're songs that have had a great impact on the Israeli psyche and Israeli culture. What is beautiful about them is that they were written by mostly Western or Eastern European composers that came in the early waves of Zionism to then-Palestine...They encountered the Eastern culture that existed here, the Arabic music and then the waves of [immigration], including the Yemenite immigrants, which my family were part of. And this East-West encounter gave birth to many beautiful songs that really reflected the emerging State of Israel and its state of mind.

Musically, the compositions are really beautiful, and the lyrics are the highest form of Hebrew poetry that exists. In that period, the Hebrew language was experiencing a renaissance. It was going from being a strictly biblical language to becoming a contemporary, vibrant, growing language. And these poets and composers were really exploring the depths of this beautiful language.

TT: But given that you were raised in the United States, were these songs you grew up with?

Noa: Actually, I did, because my parents are both Israelis, Yemenites...I grew up with quite a mix of cultures, because not only did I have a very Israeli home, but I had my Yemenite grandmother who lived with us, and she raised us. ... I grew up with these songs and Yemenite music. I also heard American music. The music of the '60s, which was the music that I loved the most, even though I was born after it. I would have loved to live in that period and have worked in that period... Leonard Cohen, Paul Simon and Joni Mitchell were all a great influence on me. [Nonetheless,] this is the first time in my career that I decided to perform these songs. I really wanted to raise them on a pedestal and so we decided to collaborate with the Jerusalem Symphony Orchestra...We called it "The Israeli Songbook," after the "Gershwin Songbook," which Ella Fitzgerald did with Nelson Riddle and all these great arrangers. We've arranged it for quartets for this show, and it will be a featured part of this program. There will also be other [songs].

TT: Did you hesitate before recording these songs, which so many Israeli artists, such as Arik Einstein, have made famous?

Noa: Yes, there was one song, for example, that we did have a lot of hesitation, called "Hayu Leilot" (There Were Nights) which everyone in Israel knows...We took another poem by Arhel, another very well-known poet of the time, put it to music and then wove the new song into the old song. We also took two very well-known children's songs, put them together and created a classic operatic aria. One of the highlights of the show [is] a medley of songs that were written about the Yemenite emigration that is very vibrant and rhythmic with percussion. We did all kinds of things to give these songs a new life.

TT: Why these songs now? My theory is that with Israel's 65th birthday, and all the societal changes that have been occurring in Israel, the time is right to remind Israeli society of songs that united them.

Noa: Yes—you can say that. Here we have the opportunity to shed light on a lesser-known corner of Israeli culture and diversity and beauty and depth. I've been performing [these songs] all over the world, and people are very intrigued by and fall in love with them.

TT: Having been a vocal peace activist in Israel and abroad, can you talk a bit about why you feel it is important to speak out as you do, and also why, as you've said elsewhere, you believe artists, even those who oppose the Israeli government, should perform in Israel rather than boycott it.

Noa: Israeli artists who perform abroad invariably carry a message of peace and of culture, and arts, above all. There are so many people in our country who believe in peace. Not everybody, maybe, but enough—not only in our country, but on the other side of the border. It's the responsibility of every human being who wants to live in peace to work for it. You can't expect people to do the work for you. … I'm a singer, so I sing for peace. I think whoever can do something, should.

As for artists boycotting Israel, I am absolutely against that. [Israel] is a pluralistic place, a diverse place. Turning your back on Israel and not playing here plays directly into the hands of the extremists, [because] people say, "You see, everybody hates us, nobody wants to come here. Let's be more defensive. Let's build more walls. Let's be more protective of what we have." Rather than [being] more embracing, more open to the international community and to international humanistic values. Not coming here is making the situation much, much worse. That's one. Second, if you do have the balls to come here as an artist, then come and say what you think. Visit this country, then go to the Palestinians and visit them and see for yourself what's going on. If you believe in peace, say it. Say it! And practice what you preach.

SOUTH AFRICAN JEWS FIND A HOME IN LA

How far can you travel in less than an hour? All the way to Capetown, South Africa, and back, if you are talking to Leora Raikin, a third-generation South African Jew who has lived in Los Angeles for the past fifteen years. Raikin will speak about the Jews of South Africa on June 18 at the Skirball Cultural Center. She will also lead several workshops on African folk art embroidery this summer, as well as serve as a visiting artist at Camp Ramah.

Raikin and her family came to Los Angeles, as did many other South African Jewish families, because they had family already living here. In Southern California in general, and in the Valley in particular, they found lots more South African Jews. "It's a close community, where we know each other, and if we don't, we certainly know people in common," Raikin said.

For South African Jews here in LA, the climate, and the topography of mountains and beaches is reminiscent of Cape Town, and Los Angeles' thriving business climate provides opportunity much like they had in Johannesburg.

"We don't live in LA because we don't like South Africans," Raikin said. Rather, they like Los Angeles because of the freedom the United States affords South African Jews, whether those who fled the apartheid regime, or those who've come recently, as the South African economy became more challenging, or because they perceive the tenor of their country becoming more anti-Israel.

Raikin says that Los Angeles' South African Jews share a common Jewish education and Jewish literacy that puts them at ease with traditional ritual, even if they are not observant. Chabad of West Hills, in particular, has become popular among South African Jews from all over the Valley, and even the Westside of Los Angeles, because it has a rabbi, Avi Rabin, who grew up in South Africa and continues to celebrate South African customs, such as holding a braai—an Afrikaans word for a barbecue—at which they serve traditional South African Jewish foods, as well as comedy nights with South African comedians.

In some ways, the story of South Africa's Jews parallels that of American Jewry: Both countries have offered refuge for Jews; for each, the greatest wave of immigration occurred from Eastern Europe at the start of the 20th century; both offered immense opportunity allowing Jews to transform themselves from a class of peddlers to industry leaders of overwhelmingly affluent communities. Yet, as Raikin explained recently, the question that has always been central to the drama of South African Jewry to this day is: "Do the Jews have a future in South Africa?"

Cape Town's first synagogue, Tikvath Israel (Hope of Israel—a reference to the Cape of Good Hope), was built in 1849.

Between 1880 and 1910, the Jewish community grew tenfold, from 4,000 to 40,000, the overwhelming majority of it Yiddish-speaking Lithuanians, including Raikin's grandparents, who hailed from Vilna.

"When my grandparents arrived, they were fortunate to still be allowed in," Raikin said. Despite the fact that many Jews fought in the Boer Wars in the 1930s, the Afrikaners and the National Party supported Nazi Germany and attempted to pass Nuremberg-type racial laws against the Jews. Although those laws failed, the government halted the immigration of European Jews after 1938.

In 1948, the National Party came to power in South Africa and passed apartheid (racial segregation) laws. Although the National Party had professed anti-Semitic polices earlier, they did not adopt these when they took power. To the contrary, they apologized to the Jewish community. Under apartheid, the Jewish community was granted all the privileges of other whites, and suffered none of the discrimination against blacks. South Africa was also one of the first countries to recognize Israel, and its premier was one of the first foreign heads of state to visit Israel, in 1953, beginning a long history of friendly relations between the countries. Even when South Africa limited what funds South Africans could send outside the country, an exception was made for donations to the State of Israel.

Many in the Jewish community disapproved of the National Party and apartheid, but rather than create conflict, they turned inward, focusing on Jewish traditions, their own community and on Israel. As Raikin explained, "It was this insulated community, [with a] very strong connection to Judaism; even if they weren't religious, they would celebrate Shabbat [on] Friday evening with their families; they would light candles; they would keep kosher in the home." At the community's peak in the 1970s, 120,000 Jews were living in South Africa, eighty percent with roots from Eastern Europe.

In the kitchen, South African Jews adopted the local flavors into their traditional Eastern European dishes, so while chopped herring was often served at festive meals, it was paired with kichlach (a thin buscuit dusted with sugar), as well as teiglach (dough cooked in honey),ingberlach (a Passover carrot or ginger candy), pletzlach (walnuts and honey), mini-pap (a maize dish), fried fish balls and per-peri (fried giblets). Raikin often serves these dishes at her lectures.

The years of apartheid were also when many Jews rose to leadership roles in several industries in South Africa, including retail, finance, real estate, insurance and health care. Among the prominent South African Jews Raikin spoke of were Harry Oppenheimer of DeBeers, the diamond company; Sol Kerzner, who founded two of South Africa's largest hotel and hospitality groups, and who developed the Mohegan Sun casino resort in Connecticut, the Atlantis Hotel and Resort in the Bahamas and the One&Only hotel chain; and Raymond Ackerman, a retailing magnate who was a partner of Raikin's great grandfather's brother.

As individuals, many Jews were among the leaders of the anti-apartheid movement. A greater percentage of the Jewish community was active in the struggle against apartheid than any other white group. Among the leaders of the movement, Joe Slovo, Albie Sachs, Ruth First and Denis Goldberg were all born Jewish, although they identified more strongly with leftist or communist political parties (Slovo, for example, headed the South African Communist Party and sat on the executive board of the African National Congress [ANC]). Oppenheimer, the chairman of the DeBeers diamond company, who was born Jewish but converted to the Anglican faith, used his influence in the business community to campaign for an end to apartheid. Helen Suzman was the only Progressive Party candidate elected to parliament and was the sole voice there unequivocally opposed to apartheid. Arthur Chaskalson and Harry Schwarz served on Nelson Mandela's defense team. Nadine Gordimer, one of South Africa's best-known writers, helped Nelson Mandela edit his speech in his own defense at the 1960s Rivonia trial for sabotage. When she won the Nobel Prize in Literature, Gordimer donated her prize money to the Congress of South African Writers. Synagogues in Johannesburg and Capetown provided support services for the black community, with nurseries, medical clinics, adult education programs and legal defense services.

The personal cost for resistance against the South African National Party was high: When Mandela was sentenced to life in prison, Goldberg, who was on trial with him, received the same sentence, as well. First was murdered. Sachs lost an eye and an arm. Attorney Rowley Arenstein was exiled for thirty-three years. Painter Arthur Goldreich was jailed. This was also true for individual students who protested against apartheid or refused military service, as many increasingly did. Lives were ruined.

In the Oscar-winning documentary *Searching for Sugar Man*, the beauty of Capetown is clearly visible, but so is the government media clampdown that made it possible for Sixto Rodriguez's songs to become so popular—while also unknown outside of South Africa.

"We all knew those [Rodriguez] songs, every single word of those songs we sang at Jewish summer camp, and we thought everyone in the world knew them," Raikin said.

"By the time I got to university, in 1988, there was a state of emergency; you couldn't gather in groups of three or more, and if you were caught disturbing or agitating in any way, you were expelled from the university and put in jail." The message was: Get your degree and leave the country or toe the line. "The activists that did stand up led very erratic lives, moving from house to house and trying not to get caught. Now they're seen as heroes, because they were trying to make changes."

Despite the actions of Jewish individuals and institutions, South Africa's Jewish Board of Deputies and the South African Rabbinate were more reluctant to stand up to the government and did not denounce apartheid until the mid-1980s. The State of Israel, for its part, was faulted for maintaining trade and military relations with the government, in violation of international trade sanctions. Israel claimed that that it was neither in the best interests of Israel nor its large community of South African Jews to be cut off and isolated.

History, however, moves at its own pace. In January 1989, entrenched Conservative President P.W. Botha had a stroke, and he was forced to resign the following month. F.W. de Klerk, also thought to be conservative, succeeded Botha, but shortly thereafter repealed the ban on political parties such as the ANC, released political prisoners not guilty of common crimes, restored press freedom and ended the death penalty. In 1990, Mandela was released from prison after twenty-seven years. Apartheid was dismantled in a series of negotiations from 1990-1993 culminating in an election, in which all South Africans could vote, that elected Mandela as president.

"It's an absolute miracle that the transition happened with so little bloodshed," Raikin now says. Raikin who had graduated the University of Cape Town with a master's degree in market research, began to work with voices of the "rainbow nation," learning and explaining the various communities to one another, which informed and expanded her understanding of African tribal art.

While Mandela himself thanked the Jewish community for its support and appointed Jews to prominent positions (his former defense attorney, Chaskalson, became Chief Justice of South Africa's Supreme Court), and even made a state visit to Israel in 1999, the ANC seemed to hold a grudge against Israel for its support of South Africa during the apartheid regime. Although the Arab nations and China continued to maintain trade relations during the same period, it was Israel that was singled out. South Africa became increasingly anti-Israel, with anti-Zionist rhetoric in the national media fanning the flames, according to Raikin.

As a result, South African Jews have continued to emigrate, with South Africa's Jewish population decreasing to 60,000-70,000. At the same time, the South African Jewish community has become more isolated and more Orthodox, with new shuls being opened by Ohr Somayach and Chabad. For Raikin, the question of "Do the Jews have a future in South Africa?" became pressing. For her, the answer is that the Jews of South Africa have a future—in Los Angeles. Three generations of her family live here now, completing a journey begun in Vilna, halfway around the world.

"We, as a family, are so grateful that we now live in a country like America that openly supports the State of Israel, that, after Israel, is the best place to be Jewish in the world."

About seven years ago, Raikin began teaching African folklore embroidery and discovered a way to tell the story of the South African people, and that of South Africa's Jews. Since then, she has taught more than 10,000 people about tribal arts and crafts, embroidering a rich thread in the quilt work that is the story of the Jewish people.

June 13, 2013

WHAT IS IT WITH ISRAELIS AND HIGH TECH?

The Israel Conference held at the Luxe Hotel on Sunset Boulevard May 30-31 was the largest gathering I've ever seen of…Israelis in suits.

Beyond that, the two-day event was a persuasive showcase of Israeli innovation and how companies from all over the world—including Procter & Gamble (P&G), IBM, and Deutsche Telekom—are opening research and development offices in Israel to bottle some of the magic of the startup nation.

Organized around a series of panels on broad subjects such as "Big Data," "Mobile Everywhere," and "Smarter Cities," the conference was punctuated by very short presentations by individual company executives of new technologies. Outside the main conference room, booths (tables, really) were set up for companies that wanted to showcase their products or new technologies. Among them was SodaStream (sodastream.com), the carbonated water dispenser that has made deals with Crystal Light, Ocean Spray and KitchenAid. (Admit it, you almost bought one at Bed Bath & Beyond!) SodaStream was the first

Israeli company to have a Super Bowl commercial and boasts one of the most successful IPOs of an Israel-based company.

Looming over the Israel Conference was the big question: Are Israeli companies best suited to just being startups that develop new technology—to be bought out by larger global companies who can better market and deploy and distribute their products—or should these companies be allowed to mature in Israel, creating jobs and industry there rather than merely for export? It's a question that made headlines with Google's recent purchase of Waze, the Israeli traffic app, for what media reports have pegged at more than $1 billion and the promise that its headquarters will remain in Israel for now.

The answer, according to speakers at the conference, was: Both. Israel must continue to be a place where research and development is paramount, bringing new technologies and products to the market (and leading to large payouts for its founders). At the same time, Israel needs to develop a mature base and infrastructure for companies to keep their businesses headquartered in Israel.

The conference, which attracted more than 600 attendees, has become a major shmoozefest. I collected some twenty-five business cards—almost all from CEOs—and that was without really trying. There were American venture capital investors, gaming executives, even some former and current Hollywood agents. This was a room full of people talking about Israel with no mention of "the situation" or "the territories" or even the Charedi. (The most politically charged conversation related to income equality created by tech execs' exit packages.)

So what is it that makes Israel so conducive to successful startups? Lital Asher-Dotan, who established P&G's Israel

House of Innovation, the company's first R&D center in Israel, spoke of the country's "culture of entrepreneurship, where everything is possible. They don't take no for an answer." Her P&G colleague, Sophie Blum, added, "Israel is global-oriented from day one, always forward-looking."

Shelley Zalis, CEO of Ipsos Open Thinking Exchange, a research firm, perhaps put it best when she said, "It's the chutzpah factor…Israel is all about, 'Act now!'"

Dov Moran, an Israeli who invented the USB flash drive, said at the conference that innovation is not hard.

"Look all around you. There are problems crying out for solutions!"

Moran explained that he got the idea for the flash drive when he was going to give a presentation and the technology failed and destroyed his presentation. After that, he vowed he would find a way to keep his presentation on him. Solutions to annoyances—that's invention, he said.

In Israel, Moran said, "There are a plethora of good ideas fueled by a [vigorous] exchange of ideas."

So, what were my takeaways from the conference, which was organized by Sharona Justman, the managing director of LA-based STEP Strategy Advisors, and co-chaired by Yossi Vardi of Israel's International Technologies (founder and seeder of more than 60 high-tech companies, including the early instant-messaging company ICQ, now sold to AOL)?

Overall, it struck me that some of the most interesting technologies are not about inventing the wheel—rather they just make the wheel roll better. So, for example, WalkMe (walkme.com) can provide online how-to guides from a company in real time as you do any task—saving companies on customer service calls, tech support and returns of merchandise. Pango (pango-parking.com), not only tells you about parking availability at public and private spaces in real time based on your location, but also incentivizes you to alert the service when are about to leave a spot by awarding points and prizes. Paperless Proposal (paperlessproposal.com) is a collaborative platform for sending presentations. (Think of it as YouSendIt for PowerPoints.)

Here are some other things I learned at the Israel Conference: Most of the 3D motion technology (à la Wii and Kinect) was developed in Israel. Procter & Gamble has an office in Israel for R&D, as does IBM, which has been there for sixty-two of Israel's sixty-five years.

Apps are an $80 billion industry (that's with a "b"), and social gaming (i.e., Words With Friends) is fifty-nine percent female and overwhelmingly mobile driven, so there is a great need for more women executives and developers.

And there are forty million dog owners in the United States, 80 percent of whom leave their pets at home for four hours or more and feel guilty about it. Wonder what that last statistic has to do with Israel? An Israeli firm is launching DogTV, the first channel of programming for dogs to watch while you're out of the house. Don't laugh (OK, it is funny) but Dish Network is going to beam DogTV (dogtv.com) into twenty million homes. So who's laughing now?

What was striking was in how many diverse fields Israelis and Israeli-developed technology are making an impact.

Ynon Kreiz, chairman of the board of one the top YouTube multichannel distribution networks and production facilities, Maker Studios (makerstudios.com), spoke of the emergence of video content as "a whole new revolution" delivered to people all over the world in real time. According to Kreiz, 100 hours of video are being uploaded every minute, and there are large fortunes to be made for small, even stupid jokes that people enjoy. (Don't believe him? Check out Snoop Lion — formerly the rapper Snoop Dogg—as Moses battling Santa in "Epic Rap Battles of History").

In medical science, there were presentations from OraMed (www.oramed.com), which focuses on the oral delivery of medicines such as insulin; SureTouch (suretouch.us), maker of a new, simpler device for breast exams; and Dario (mydario.com), a diabetes management system.

In a panel on "Smarter Cities," we got a look at Israeli company Mer Systems' (mer-systems.com) control room for city-wide security and communication, which is being tested in Buenos Aires; and CanarIT, an inexpensive multisensor air quality monitoring system from AirBase (myairbase.com).

Finally, there were some technologies I simply can't wait to use. There was Tako (tako.com), a Dropbox for apps, which Ross Avner, co-founder and the former head of Yahoo! Games, says will be out of stealth mode in 2014 and which will allow you to access any of your apps on any of your devices or home screens. Appeo (appeo.com) is a virtual services market that works 24/7 (there are several demos on YouTube). It will allow you both to have professional services performed, such as drafting a will or translating a document, and set up a virtual company providing those services. Then there's Magisto (magisto.com), an online video editing software that brings Instagram-like simplicity to making your videos look more professional.

I was particularly taken with Wibbitz (wibbitz.com), software that converts text into videos (i.e., you could be watching this article rather than reading it). Imagine that a search engine was automatically reading the article and grabbing images to go with it, while a voice-to-text software reads it.

And I am curious to see Moran's latest project, Comigo (comigo.com), an operating system that the flash drive inventor feels will not only topple Microsoft and Google but, in his words, "change the world."

No one at the Israel Conference even blinked an eye when Moran made that ambitious, impossible-seeming prediction — not the American software and gaming executives in the room, not the venture capitalists and investors mingling outside, eating Israeli food or listening to the music of Steve Katz. It was a room in which, like proud Jewish parents, it was OK to boast, as if everyone there was family.

"What other conference," co-chair Vardi asked, "serves pickles on all the tables?"

June 19, 2013

HANS RICHTER'S FUTURE IS NOW!

The exhibition "Hans Richter: Encounters" at the Los Angeles County Museum of Art is a curator's dream: retrospective of a somewhat obscure, multiplatform artist, who is equally adept (and revolutionary) in painting and film; whose life and career intersects with the major artists and artistic movements of the 20th century; and whose work, when organized didactically, continues to appear very of the moment, ready for reappraisal and for greater attention.

Although the show's curator, Timothy O. Benson, had written about Richter in the 1990s, he was surprised when contacted about eight years ago by the curator of Richter's estate, Erik de Bourbon-Parme, to work on a possible exhibition in cooperation with curators at the Centre Georges Pompidou in Paris. During Richter's lifetime (1888-1976), as described in his memoir "Encounters From Dada Till Today," which LACMA has republished as an e-book, Richter managed in Zelig-like fashion to befriend a wide range of artists and filmmakers, including Hans Arp, Jean Cocteau, George Méliès, Joseph Cornell, Piet Mondrian, Sergei Eisenstein, Marcel Duchamp, Man Ray, Federico Fellini, Fernand Léger, Alexander Calder, Kazimir Malevich and Fritz Lang, among many others whom he influenced and who influenced him. Benson wanted to honor Richter's talents as an artist but also, in Benson's words, as "innovator-director-collaborator-organizer-instigator-facilitator-transmitter–curator and chronicler." This approach makes particular sense at LACMA, whose director, Michael Govan, has championed exhibitions that highlight the artistic dimension of filmmakers (Tim Burton and Stanley Kubrick, among them) as well as artists who have made films (Dali, and now Richter).

At LACMA, "Hans Richter: Encounters," whose installation has been designed by the architectural firm Frederick Fisher and Partners, the central core of Richter's film work, projected on exhibit room walls, becomes the spine of the exhibition, from which emanate nine rooms of art and objects by Richter and other artists that give context to Richter's work and influence.

Johannes Siegfried (Hans) Richter was born to a well-off German-Jewish family in 1888 (his mother was a Rothschild). He studied at the Academy of Art in Berlin and the Academy of Art in Weimar. As a teenager, he began drawing portraits of family members. Early exposure to the Blue Rider group of painters led by Franz Marc and the German Expressionists can be seen in these early works, some of which appeared in the Berlin avant-garde intellectual publications such as Die Aktion and Der Sturm. With the advent of Cubism, Richter saw how abstract forms could express an artistic, or even utopian, vision.

In 1914, shortly after the outbreak of World War I, Richter was drafted and seriously wounded outside Vilnius, Lithuania. A younger brother died in the war, and another was wounded.

Richter returned to Berlin with a greater commitment to political change, envisioning the power of art to be a force for radicalism. If the world war was meant to be "the war to end all wars," Richter increasingly believed that a better world was possible, one without militarism where radical art could be a transformative force in society. For the rest of his life, Richter sought out the radical in his art.

As luck would have it, Richter was not alone in his views. At a café in Zurich, Switzerland, he was introduced by a friend to Tristan Tzara (Samy Rosenstock), with whom he would become involved in the Dada movement, through which Richter would make lifelong friends with Duchamp and Ray (Emmanuel Radnitzky). Richter formed the Radical Artists Group after the Russian Revolution in 1917. Tzara introduced Richter to the Swedish artist Viking Eggeling, with whom Richter began to collaborate, creating visual scrolls that were "contrapuntal" and resembled musical scores, exploring notions of duality, of the power of opposites such as black and white, positive and negative, not only in drawings and painting but also particularly in experimental film. In 1921, Richter made what is considered one of the first abstract films, *Rhythmus 21*.

Richter knew many of the early film innovators, including Méliès and Eisenstein. But it was Richter's status as an artist that set him apart as a filmmaker. When Kazimir Malevich, the Russian Suprematist painter, wanted to collaborate on a film, he chose Richter over Eisenstein because he felt Richter would be able to move the art of film forward. Richter very much saw his role as being part of the avant-garde, "Not to just roll up his sleeves and just make something, but to listen for the future. He felt like the future was something in formation that the artist could hear," Benson said.

It may be hard to appreciate today, but abstract art and film were once revolutionary. To Richter, however, abstraction represented both the intellectual and the human side of art—a purity of form and design that transcended borders and could be accepted as a universal language. "I see him as an instigator and leader," Benson said.

In the 1920s, Richter launched the art journal Periodical G, whose full title was G: Materials for Elemental Form Creation. Inspired by Theo van Doesburg's De Stijl, G gathered such diverse talents as artist El Lissitzky and designer Ludwig Mies van der Rohe, on architecture, industrial design, city planning, typography, painting and film. "I see him as the Miles Davis of the art world," Benson said, "because he listens and he knows which people to put together to make something happen at a particular time."

In 1929, Richter was called upon to use his gregarious social talents to organize the "Film und Foto" exhibition that traveled throughout Europe, including to Stuttgart, Berlin, Zurich and Vienna, featuring the work of his friends and contemporaries, among them Laszlo Moholy-Nagy, Hannah Höch, Léger, Ray, and Duchamp. Nonetheless, during the 1930s it became increasingly clear that while Richter did not consider himself particularly Jewish, the Nazis did. Richter's work was included in the infamous Nazi exhibition "Degenerate Art," and the artist was forced to leave Germany in 1933 for the more hospitable environs of Southern France and Switzerland. As the 1930s came to end, he sought refuge in the United States but could not get a visa despite his friendships and contacts. According to Benson, it was only through the intervention of the Hebrew Immigrant Aid Society that Richter was allowed into the United States, where he joined the faculty of the City University of New York to chair its film department.

New York was awash in European émigré artists, and Richter found himself renewing old friendships with Duchamp and Ray, and making new ones with Jonas Mekas, Maya Deren, Joseph Cornell and John Cage. He returned to painting, making large scrolls that revisited old work and made the imagery new, adding elements of amorphous shapes as counterpoints and introducing elements of collage. He also made films, including the feature "Dreams That Money Can Buy." In the 1960s, he adopted the format of working in series, using a variety of abstract forms and materials to explore his ideas.

Richter died in 1976. However, as an art figure, his use of so many different media, his way of collaborative working, his publications such as G, make him seem very of the moment. As Benson explained, "Like many artists today, he moves from one medium to the next, almost effortlessly…He often did things that are very short, ten-minute or a three-minute film sequence, and young people work that way now. He's also a social-media person. He had his own social networks. Those aspects really make him of our time."

For Richter, an artist who always set himself at the cutting edge of his time, his sought-for future is now.

July 2, 2013

LUSTING FOR LEICAS

In one version of our lives, childhood is a series of deprivations and desires whereby we want things we can't have, some of which we grow out of or just forget. In my case, I was seized with heartache when I entered the newly opened 8,000-square-foot Leica store on Beverly Boulevard at Robertson in West Hollywood. Until then, I had forgotten how much I wanted to own a Leica.

Leica is the 100-year-old optics company founded by Ernst Leitz in Wetzlar, Germany, known originally as the Leitz Camera Co. (shortened to LEICA). The company became well known for making the first 35mm film camera, and for its rangefinder, variable lens system and for the quality of its lenses. The camera was the favorite of many professional photographers, such as Henri Cartier-Bresson and Alfred Eisenstaedt, the latter of whom used a Leica to shoot his famous picture of a sailor kissing a girl in Times Square. Today, the company is based in Solms, Germany, and Andreas Kaufmann, a German national who resides in Austria, is the majority shareholder.

My own passion for photography and for cameras was kindled by a summer job, at thirteen, in a midtown Manhattan camera store run by Hungarian Jewish émigrés. Back then, there was a hierarchy to everything, including desire. The serious young photographer graduated from taking snapshots to a single-lens reflex camera, such as a Mamiya Sekor (popular among my friends), or, if you were more affluent, a Pentax. From there you graduated to an Olympus, and then a Nikon. Professionals used professional versions of the Nikon—which were all black. For the truly discerning, however, the object of desire was the Leica.

The Leica felt solid and was fully manual (a plus to the camera geek), allowing for maximum choice, and therefore, maximum artistic control in each photo. It sat in your hand with a satisfying heft, a solidness that spoke to its seriousness of purpose. To me, it was the embodiment of the schwarzgerat (literally "the black device"), a finely tooled exemplar of German engineering so satisfying in its design and manufacture, so intelligently made, that its use gave pleasure and conferred status and excellence on the user. The reverence in which the schwarzgerat is held has been central to several contemporary classics such as the black monolith in Stanley Kubrick's *2001* or the secret component in the searched-for rocket in Thomas Pynchon's *Gravity's Rainbow*. I aspired to the Leica, although I knew it was way out of my league.

Everything about it said "German," which might have added to its forbidden-fruit status, as my parents, Holocaust memories ever fresh, didn't buy German. However, just as the overwhelming quality of the product convinced some Jews to drive Mercedeses and BMWs, particularly after Israel accepted the wiedergutmachung—reparations from Germany—Leica was adopted by many Jewish photographers, among them Robert Capa and Cornell Capa.

Jewish guilt was further assuaged by an e-mail that has been making the rounds for the last several years (I've received it as least three times from three different sources), variously referred to as "Leica and the Jews" or "The Leica Freedom Train." The e-mail tells of how, as the Nazis came to power, Ernst Leitz II, son of the founder, arranged for his Jewish employees to leave Germany. He strung Leicas over their necks and dubbed them Leica sales agents, allowing them to obtain travel visas when those were increasingly hard to get. The cameras themselves served as proof and were a valuable commodity upon arrival in a foreign land. In many cases, Leitz personally arranged introductions to photo businesses in the United States and other countries for his employees. This continued until 1939, when Germany closed its borders to all Jews. Even after that, Leitz's daughter was involved in helping to smuggle Jews into Switzerland. As Protestants, Leitz said, it was just the right thing to do and he never sought any acclaim for his actions.

A spirit more truculent than mine might point out that Leica did not close its factories under the Reich, or move its operations to the United States or England—to the contrary, Leica optics were very valuable to the German war effort, and Leitz remained a Nazi party member. And although the company was never convicted of using slave labor, in 1988 it voluntarily paid into a fund set up for German companies to compensate former slave laborers. But this does not make what Leica did for its Jewish employees prior to 1939 any less true: Those "Leica Jews," their children, grandchildren and great-grandchildren are alive because of the opportunity Leitz gave them.

As cameras became increasingly automated, Leica continued to focus on its manual attributes; as digital cameras entered the marketplace, Leica was slow to join the parade. However, in the past few years, they have introduced increasingly sophisticated digital products worthy of the Leica name, and the brand seems to be making a comeback.

For many years, though, Leica had been off my radar. Then I walked into the Leica megastore, a gleaming cube, replete with an upstairs gallery space showing the works of celebrated portrait photographer Mary Ellen Mark, Seal (yes, the singer, who is a brand ambassador for the company, as well as an accomplished photographer with special access to nude models lying on hotel room beds) and Yariv Milchan, the landscape and celebrity photographer (whose Hollywood connection is genetic—his father is entertainment mogul Arnon Milchan). It also houses a bookstore selling rare and well-chosen photo books, curated by Martin Parr of Magnum. And, finally, there are the cameras.

There is much to lust for: The store sells the full range of Leicas, from point-and-shoot cameras that will fit in your pocket ($700-$800), to the legendary M series, featuring its M lens mount first introduced in 1954, to special collaborations with G-Star Raw Denim and Hermes leather, some of which cost as much as $7,500. There is even a monochrome digital camera for taking high-resolution images in black and white that would be a worthy addition to any serious photographer's camera bag.

I met with James Agnew, the store's general manager, and Annie Seaton, the gallery's manager, and asked them, "Why a Leica store in LA? Why now?"

"It's the right time for Leica, the right time for Los Angeles." Agnew said, "Los Angeles is an increasingly important center for the arts. It is an exciting time for photography in Los Angeles."

Seaton added: "I think of Los Angeles as the home of the moving image. Where else to start but in Hollywood?"

In some ways, one might think this would be the worst possible time to be selling expensive cameras. In the last few years, images made using smartphones and iPhones posted on Instagram, Snapchat and Facebook have made everyone a photographer or a photodiarist of their meals, pets, friends and selves. Hasn't digital and the Internet disrupted and leveled photography?

Agnew sees it differently. He believes the ubiquity of photos has created a backlash, and he believes there is "overall a return to the tradition of photography and a renewed call for quality cameras and images." The Leica store is there not only to celebrate photography but also photographs: It will offer full printing services, in addition to repair service and sales.

What became clear from talking with Agnew—who prior to opening this new Leica store, worked for such luxury retailers as Giorgio Armani, Chanel, and Van Cleef & Arpels—is that Leica is positioning itself as a luxury company. We live in a society where driving a Bentley rather than a Prius (or, rather, driving a Bentley in addition to a Prius) is a choice that the marketplace supports. So, for every 1,000 or 10,000 iPhone photo enthusiasts, there will be some who crave, or succumb to, the quality and the allure of a Leica.

And if they can't afford one, then, like me, they can spend time at the beautiful new Leica megastore, lusting for excellence.

September 3, 2013

MOSHE SADFIE: THE PEOPLE'S ARCHITECT

The Skirball Cultural Center, which stands at the crest of Sepulveda and Mulholland just west of the 405 Freeway, was built on a dump. Literally. Who knew? Before the Skirball acquired the land, it was a garbage dump. With its opening in 1996, architect Moshe Safdie, in his first commission in the United States, transformed the site into a campus of concrete and granite pavilions, set into the hills, following the curves of the river of traffic that runs through the Sepulveda Pass.

Designed to be built in phases, as visitors and needs arose (and as funds were raised), the Skirball has extended over the past three decades to the south with the additions of Winnick Hall and Noah's Ark, and to the north with Ahmanson Hall, and now finds completion with the Herscher Hall and Guerin Pavilion, to be unveiled this fall. The design for the new buildings fits seamlessly with the older ones, as if it were always there just waiting to be built. Its walls of windows afford beautiful vistas of the hills, and, inside, it contains a 9,000-square-foot multiuse hall, a 4,000-square-foot kitchen, and meeting rooms ready for a class, a screening or even a Korean tea ceremony.

While the completion of this fourth and final phase of Safdie's Skirball campus is cause enough for celebration, the exhibition "Global Citizen: The Architecture of Moshe Safdie," which opens Oct. 22, will excavate the singular career of the Israeli-born architect who holds passports from Israel, Canada and the United States. Perhaps best known for his design for Yad Vashem, Safdie's name has been counted among the top of the list of the many great architects of our time, such as Frank Gehry, Jean Nouvel, Richard Meier, and I. M. Pei.

The exhibition was originated at the National Gallery of Canada in 2010, organized by Donald Albrecht, curator of architecture and design at the Museum of the City of New York.

"The exhibition is called 'Global Citizen' not only because Safdie is a citizen of the United States, Canada and Israel," Albrecht explained recently, "but because his architecture projects all over the world…bring diverse people together." As Albrecht notes in the catalog, it is "Safdie's intention to use architecture not only to express, but also to generate, open engagement in community life."

Organized chronologically, the exhibition includes models of some of Safdie's best-known works in Canada (Habitat 67 and the National Gallery of Canada in Ottawa), in the United States (the Skirball, the Salt Lake City Public Library, Crystal Bridges Museum of American Art), in Israel (Yad Vashem, the Mamilla Alrov Center, a multiuse urban center near the Old City of Jerusalem, and Ben-Gurion Airport) and elsewhere (among others, the Khalsa Heritage Center of Sikh culture in Punjab, India, and the planned Jumilla Mosque in Dubai). The show also includes designs for projects and entries for architectural competitions that were never built, as well as films that will be screened in the galleries to give a sense of the experience of interacting with the three-dimensional built spaces.

The exhibition organizes Safdie's career into several phases. To begin with, he was born in Haifa in 1938, and the mix there of cultures and religions, as well as the proliferation of modernist stacked housing on Mount Carmel, had a profound influence on him, all the more so because his family moved to Montreal in 1953. Memories of Haifa can be seen in Safdie's groundbreaking undergraduate architecture thesis at McGill University, a design for a modular building system using prefabricated forms fashioned into stacks of individual homes with terraced gardens, which would become Montreal's Habitat 67 (one of the prefab molded bathrooms is showcased in the exhibition). Meant to be scaled for a variety of locales (Manhattan, Puerto Rico and Tehran), Habitat never was built beyond its initial Montreal development. Indeed, in the years that immediately followed Habitat's completion, Safdie's work met with resistance, as can be seen with his unsuccessful submissions for the student union at San Francisco State University, and for Paris' Centre Pompidou, both of which went to other architects.

Safdie returned to Israel following the Six-Day War to complete his military service, and in 1970 moved to Jerusalem, where he opened an office. This began the second phase of his career, notable for projects at the Hebrew Union College campus, the beginning of his work on the Mamilla complex and at Yad Vashem. In these, we see the emergence of the elements of Safdie's distinctive architectural vocabulary, all profoundly influenced by Jerusalem's Old City: his mixing of concrete, stone and granite, which allow the architecture to fade to the background, highlighting instead light-filled passageways, either open-air or skylight-enhanced, and a predominance of simple geometric forms in the buildings, as well as the walkways, plazas and gardens.

The third phase of Safdie's career extends his work to North America, and can be seen in his consistent selection as designer of significant cultural centers, including the Skirball in Los Angeles; the National Gallery of Canada in Ottawa; the Exploration Place Science Center in Wichita, Kansas; the Peabody Essex Museum in Salem, Mass.; the Salt Lake City Public Library in Utah; the United States Institute of Peace headquarters in Washington, D.C.; and Crystal Bridges Museum of American Art in Bentonville, Ark. Striking in all these endeavors is how they all are designed to be enjoyed by a large and diverse stream of visitors. The other striking feature is that with the exception of the National Gallery of Canada, whose glass structure echoes Ottawa's landmark towers, Safdie's designs generally do not call attention to themselves. They continue, in this phase, his use of geometrical forms derived from nature but greatly abstracted (sometimes by benefit of computer design). The buildings harmonize with their surroundings rather than stand out, and they are not afraid to be grand, but are incomplete without the presence of people interacting with their spaces. And, it is important to note, Safdie's public projects have been overwhelmingly popular. Salt Lake City's library has been called "America's unquietest library," and the Crystal Bridges Museum, commissioned by Walmart heiress Alice Walton and opened in 2011, has exceeded all projections for attendance.

The fourth and current phase of Safdie's practice is an increasingly global one, with the Khalsa center in India, the Marina Bay Sands complex in Singapore (commissioned by Sheldon Adelson), and proposals for the Guangdong Science Center in China and the Palm Jumeirah Gateway Mosque in Dubai. These are monumental projects, and for them Safdie's architectural statements, particular in the Khalsa center, are bolder. Yet they retain his trademark order and elegance—no Gehry-esque dissonant clash of squiggly lines for Safdie.

While some architects' designs for museums and buildings make the outside more famous than what's inside, Safdie's work is different: His architecture often takes a back seat to its surroundings and to its purpose, whether residential, or public space, or multipurpose. Safdie aims to accommodate a jumble of people flowing smoothly through a variety of experiences.

What "Global Citizen: The Architecture of Moshe Safdie" does is make us appreciate his artfulness in doing so.

September 6, 2013

REMEMBERING RABBI BERG

The death on Sept. 16 of Rabbi Philip Berg, eighty-six, who founded the Kabbalah Centre with his second wife, Karen, did not come as a surprise. Rav Berg, as he was known at the center, had suffered a stroke in 2004 and had been little heard of since. Yet his legacy remains significant: In the last twenty years, the Kabbalah Centre International, headquartered on Robertson Boulevard, has opened branded centers and study groups all over the world, offering courses, books and merchandise that are based, they said, on the sacred medieval mystical texts known as the kabbalah. For these goods and services, the Centre charges fees ($180 for a course of ten lectures; $360 for a set of the books of the Zohar; $26 for a red string; $6 for kabbalah water); it also solicits donations, which have brought to the Kabbalah Centre—and the Bergs—untold millions. And they have popularized the kabbalah—once both exclusive and esoteric—to the point that it is regular fodder in the pages of *People* magazine.

Kabbalah first emerged sometime in the 12th to 13th centuries, but traditionally was not known outside a small circle of

Jewish scholars and rabbis, and has over the years, drawn a decidedly mixed reaction. Gershom Scholem, the great scholar of Jewish mysticism said: "If one turns to the writings of the great Kabbalists one seldom fails to be torn between alternate admiration and disgust...[for] the simultaneous presence of crudely primitive modes of thought and feeling and of ideas [of] profound contemplative mysticism..." The Bergs, however, found in kabbalah an ontology to base a behavioral results-oriented spiritual system useful in contemporary society, offering both mystery and systems for controlling one's self as well as, they claimed, one's destiny. They attracted the devotion of celebrities such as Madonna, Demi Moore, Ashton Kutcher, Roseanne Barr and Britney Spears, all of whom signaled their adherence by wearing a simple red string around their wrist. The Bergs also triggered the return of a number of individuals and families, including my own, to religion in general, and Judaism in particular.

In the mid-1990s, for a two- or three-year period, my wife and I were part of a group of a half dozen or more couples of varying faiths who took a series of courses sponsored by the Kabbalah Centre. Like a book club, we met weekly at a group member's home, shared a potluck dinner, then listened to a lecture by a teacher from the Kaballah Centre. Our teacher was Eitan Yardeni, who had met Rabbi Berg in Israel as a teenager and was an integral part of the Centre. We attended occasional services at the temple—for Rosh Chodesh (the beginning of each month, a big deal), for Purim (a big party). We also went to Palm Springs one year to the Riviera Hotel, where the Kabbalah Centre offered Rosh Hashanah services. On several occasions, we met Rabbi and Karen Berg, and heard each of them give both sermons and informal talks. Rabbi Berg blessed my infant daughter and her Hebrew name, Netanya (gift from God).

The Kabbalah Centre's teachings could be reduced to, "Let there be light." The Centre teaches that our individual actions matter and that it is our spiritual mission to increase the light in our lives, in our community and in the world by being a beacon for the light. This light is channeled by sharing, through good deeds, by prayer, observance and charity. It was not hard to see why this message would be of value to celebrities, among others, for whom success provided no roadmap to happiness or a meaningful life.

Another mainstay of the Centre's teachings is that when one is faced with a challenge, a problem, a decision, one should not act "reactively" (emotionally) but should "restrict" to allow the light in, and for the correct answer to emerge from our consciousness. "Restrict" is smart advice (think before you act), and one that my wife and I use to this day.

Even one of the Centre's most derided practices, "scanning" (i.e. passing your fingers over, or looking at) Hebrew text that you can't understand, was not without value. It allows one to participate in prayer, be comfortable in a setting where others are reading Hebrew and to engage with the text—even when it is foreign to you.

There was a warm feeling in having a group of friends putting aside time to reflect about our lives, our issues and how we could be better people. For a group of people, such as my wife, who grew up Jewish-Lite and didn't necessarily see the why of religion, kabbalah promised personal benefits. Standing for a religious ceremony, or a festive meal, at the Robertson Centre with a group of friends and strangers, many of them dressed in all white, provided a feeling of belonging to something, being part of something—a feeling that perhaps we didn't even know we craved.

Rabbi Berg, in person, did not strike me as a particularly spellbinding speaker, deep thinker or charismatic personality, yet he had a beatific look that radiated that quality the Kabbalah Center trumpeted—the light. Karen, by contrast, was much more engaging, down-to-earth, personable and funny.

If you were to ask me if the Kabbalah Centre is a cult, Jewish Scientology or a bastardized version of the Jewish religion, or did the Bergs seem to enjoy the trappings of success perhaps too much—the short answer is that the Kabbalah Centre is what you make of it, and while any of the aforementioned critiques may be true, in part, they seemed less so to our group. In the end, what bothered many of us was the greater involvement the Centre demanded. It was not only that they charged so much for every piece of string, book and bottle of water, but that they encouraged us to pledge allegiance to the Centre over all other places of worship, and to contribute to the Centre above all other worthy recipients.

Once Eitan was no longer our teacher (he left us for Madonna, among others), our group disbanded. Yet it is impressive, the extent to which each of us went on to greater involvement and commitment to our respective religious institutions. Almost all are today church or synagogue members (even one temple board member). For my wife, kabbalah was a bridge to Jewish thought and observance, one that led her to the congregation to which we now belong. For me, who had a more traditional Jewish education, it was an opening to the Jewish mystical tradition. For us, and the members of our group, the

Kabbalah Centre turned out to be but a way station on our spiritual journey. In the end, is that such a bad thing?

Rabbi Berg is survived by his wife Karen and the two sons of their marriage, Michael and Yehuda, all of whom remain involved in the stewardship of the Kabbalah Centre, as well as those children still extant from his first marriage.

October 9, 2013

ISRAELI WRITER ETGAR KERET ON THE LONG AND (VERY) SHORT OF IT

Etgar Keret, with his collections *The Nimrod Flip-Out* and the recently published *Suddenly, a Knock on the Door*, reinvigorated the short story (and the short, short story). The author, whose work has appeared in *The New Yorker*, Zoetrope, and on *This American Life*, recently spent a day in Los Angles, at UCLA, as a guest of the Israel Studies department, and at a reception in his honor at the home of Sharon Nazarian, president of the Younes and Soraya Nazarian Foundation, which sponsored the event.

Keret, forty-six, explained that he sees himself as more "a Jewish writer than an Israeli one," because being Jewish, he said, "is my heritage." Being Israeli, he said, as a national identity, is like "a tenant's meeting in an apartment complex: You all live together, but what do you have in common?" Keret said his kinship with Jewish writers includes the likes of Franz Kafka, Sholem Aleichem, Isaac Babel and Isaac Bashevis Singer.

Yet, he could not be more Israeli. Keret has lived his whole life in Tel Aviv. His parents were Holocaust survivors from Belarus and Poland (his father died last year). His brother was tried and convicted for deserting the Israeli army for being a pagan and staged his first marriage as a performance art event, to which he sold tickets, and his second in a tree in Thailand. Keret's sister, meanwhile, belongs to an ultra-Orthodox community and has five children.

Keret wrote his first short stories during his compulsory military service. Describing himself as a "horrible soldier," who came from a long line of horrible soldiers, he managed to be assigned to a basement computer room, where he served twenty-four- to thirty-six-hour shifts. And while there, he wrote. He said he suppresses many of his emotions, but he described fiction as, for him, "a safe zone" where he can take his anger and other feelings to unexpected places. Fiction is "a place of authenticity," where he need not lie—there are no consequences as there might be in the real world.

At the end of a very long day, Keret sat for a conversation, an edited version of which follows:

Tom Teicholz: The writers you admire, their works are all somewhat different than their reputation: Kafka is more modern and more funny; Aleichem is a master of satire on the level of Mark Twain; Babel is also funny and quite clever; and Singer is both funnier and darker, more macabre, than he is usually given credit for. So, how is your work different from how it's usually perceived?

Etgar Keret: Different people ascribe different things to [my work]. I remember when I first published my book, I went to a big conference and did a reading, where some people laughed, and others were very angry…There is always this cocktail between the text and the reader. If you mix with water, you get something else...For me, the humor is an affect, armor to protect me from other things, and the core is something that is much more painful.

TT: The other quality that distinguishes these writers is that their writing is very specific as to place but is considered universal. Is that true of your work as well?

EK: I'm forty-six years old, and my whole life I've lived in five places—all in Tel Aviv or Ramat Gan [a suburb of Tel Aviv], all within a radius of five kilometers. I'm like Kant: All my life I've lived in the same place, walked down the same streets. My best friend, I've known him since I'm three. His father came to fix our TV and didn't have a babysitter so he brought him along. I still see him every week. I'm like those Southern writers, who write about their town...As I said at the UCLA event, [when] you touch upon something that is a trait of a person, that is universal. You just have to zoom in enough.

TT: In your new collection *Suddenly, a Knock on the Door*, there's a story, "Creative Writing," in which you describe a creative writing teacher as having published a collection of stories that were "kind of a gimmick." Is that a reference to criticism you've received?

EK: I write short stories, and publishers don't like short stories. They are always coming up with ideas [like]: Write [a collection of] short stories and the character in one begins with A, and the other will be B. Or how about you write short stories [where] each story takes place in another city in Israel? It always seemed like a very bull---- idea to me so I integrated it [into the story].

TT: How do you see your stories as different from other Israeli fiction?

EK: I think, traditionally, Israeli writers tell the story of the group, of the collective. You have the kibbutz stories, the army stories—basically [you] take these people who come from different countries and try to create a whole out of them. In that sense, when I started writing, I felt that there was a kind of resentment from [the] older generation of readers and writers. Like, 'We're trying to put something together and you're working against us."

TT: That you're drawing outside the lines?

EK: Yes.

TT: In what way did your parents being Holocaust survivors make you a writer: Do you see yourself as the witness, the translator of modern experience, and/or the entertainer creating a salve or distraction from their pain?

EK: When I was a child, there was this thing that I would never cry if my parents were around. My mother saw her mother killed before her eyes. So it seemed like nothing that I had justified [crying]. I can remember that the most important thing was to make them happy. But my parents were happy people; they liked to celebrate.

This idea of not showing emotion is something that is very, very strong, and there is something about writing that is, for me, is very, very much linked to suppression of emotion [that] I have to put somewhere. I remember being a soldier and having this fear—it wasn't about showing my emotion, it was that I was afraid that I won't know what I feel—that I suppressed it so deep that I wouldn't know if I'm angry or sad. And there's something about writing that releases that.

TT: You were born shortly after the Six-Day War. In what way does that make what you write about Israel different from the writers who came before you?

EK: The [19]67 generation, we grew up in the years where Israel was like the most popular country in the world—they did the Entebbe movie with Charles Bronson; we won Miss Universe; we won [the] Eurovision [song contest] two years in a row. We were loved by everybody -— our basketball team won the European championship, and there was this feeling that we were like this wonder. During those years, Swedish girls would come [to Tel Aviv] hoping to find Israeli boyfriends.

TT: Tel Aviv has changed so much in the last decade, even in the last five years—it has a vibrant art scene, it's become a foodie haven and is known as the gay party capital of the world. Is it still your Tel Aviv? Or is it changing too fast for you?

EK: When you go to New York, you see it's the museum of the 20th century, the same way that Paris is the museum of the 19th century…What's very strong about Tel Aviv, unlike Jerusalem, is that it's a city that's constantly searching for its identity. It's almost like there is a polemic about what this city is all about…At times I feel closer and at times I feel more distant. The only other city I can compare it to is Berlin, because there's something about Jewish identity and German identity where we are not completely at ease with our identities, with saying. "This is what we are." I think Germans and Israelis are the only people I know that when their national anthems plays, they're against it…Identity issues are very central. Even though no one ever speaks about it, it's always in the subtext.

October 30, 2013

LOU ADLER: LOW KEY, LUCKY AND VERY COOL

About a mile north of Duke's in Malibu, a right turn takes you up to a bluff with its own driveway, which leads to a large parking lot. There, on the day I visited, a tour bus was parked in front of a modest ranch house, alongside several other cars, none of them too fancy. The front door was open, and I walked in unannounced, past stacks of books and vinyl records, and walls lined with posters from albums, movies and concerts. Beyond was a large living room overlooking a pool, and, beyond that the most amazing views of the Pacific Ocean. A bunch of people were milling around, seemingly working there. The house itself didn't seem like much—it could have been either a teardown, given Malibu real-estate prices, or a midcentury relic.

It is, in fact, the office of legendary music producer Lou Adler, and its lack of pretention is, I discovered, much like Adler himself: down-to-earth, casual and extremely cool.

Adler, who turns eighty in December, was finally inducted this year into the Rock and Roll Hall of Fame. He also made a cameo appearance in the wonderful new documentary about backup singers, *20 Feet From Stardom*. More than most, he has earned the title of living legend, having written songs with Herb Alpert and Sam Cooke, perhaps most notably "What a Wonderful World" (with the stick-in-your-head lyric, "Don't know much about history"), produced records for the Mamas and the Papas and Carole King (including the record-breaking 1971 album *Tapestry*, which won four Grammys, among them Album of the Year), and for the iconic comedians Cheech and Chong. He also produced the Monterey Pop Festival as well as classic films such as *The Rocky Horror Picture Show* and Cheech and Chong's *Up in Smoke* (which he also directed), and he owns the Roxy on the Sunset Strip.

Despite all this, as he freely admits, he is best known today "as the guy with the hat and the white beard who sits next to Jack Nicholson at the Lakers." Which suits him just fine.

Adler was born in 1933 on Chicago's West side but arrived in Los Angeles with his parents at eighteen months, settling in Boyle Heights. Eventually his grandparents, as well as his uncles and aunts, would all join the family in Boyle Heights. He recalls the gatherings on Friday nights at his grandparents' home: the Sabbath was celebrated with wine but no prayers. He celebrated his bar mitzvah in the Breed Street Shul.

His mother, Josie, was only sixteen when Adler was born and had left school after the eighth grade. Yet she was clearly the emotional center of Adler's life. In his Hall of Fame acceptance speech, he called her his best friend. "She was just someone who was real easy to talk to," Adler recalled. His friends, girlfriends, whoever, all fell under her spell. "She was just really special to anyone who ever met her."

By high school, Adler was, by his own account, "always looking for ways to make money." He had a job soliciting newspaper subscriptions and doing telephone marketing. However, joining the Navy at seventeen became his unlikely financial bonanza. "I was in charge of information and education," Adler said, "So I sold diplomas for $50…There are a lot of people walking around with diplomas who might not have [earned] them. I was also in charge of films, so I could make a deal—sometimes a ship went without a film because I sold the film to another ship."

Adler met his first business partner at Los Angeles City College—through Sharon Mae Lubin, whom he'd once dated. At that time, Lubin's boyfriend had been away in the Army, but when her boyfriend returned, Lubin fixed up Adler with her best friend, and the two couples double dated. Adler had always written poems and school songs, and Lubin's boyfriend was a trumpeter with a band that played at bar mitzvahs and weddings, so they decided to form a songwriting team. Whether this was the start of Adler's eye for spotting talent or dumb luck can be forever debated, but that trumpeter, whom Adler still calls "Herbie," was Herb Alpert. They called their company Herb B. Lou Productions (a word play on Desilu productions – the B. being a reference to famed KFWB disk jockey B. Mitchel Reed—who was born Burton Mitchel Goldberg).

Alpert and Adler cut four demos, with Alpert singing. They couldn't get into Columbia or RCA records, so they went instead to the small labels, whose offices were all near Hollywood and Vine, some in storefronts. And that is how they ended up at Keen Records, a label founded in Los Angeles in 1957 as a side business for John and Alex Siamas, who, were successful aerospace and aviation businessmen, along with Bob Keane (later of Del-Fi Records), who left the label in its first year.

Bandleader and producer Robert "Bumps" Blackwell was Keen's A&R man, and he hired Alpert and Adler as "assistant A&R men" for $40 a week each. "He pretty much sent us through school," Adler said, "taught us how to break down a song, how to listen to stacks of demos, what's the right chorus, what's the right verse, when do you go to the hook, all those things Herbie had some knowledge of, having been a musician."

Graduate school was provided by Cooke, one of Keen's artists. "He taught me how to communicate with musicians," said Adler, who became very close with Cooke, even becoming his roommate. Cooke also helped Adler and Alpert write one of their greatest hits. "Herb and I started a song with 'Wonderful World' in the title," Adler recalled, "with the idea of you didn't have to be educated to be a lover." Cooke suggested the song be "more of a teenage thing, more of a high school thing—instead of 'you don't need a book to be a lover,' you don't need to know algebra." The result, often referred to as "Don't know much about history," became a hit for Cooke, and then for Herman's Hermits, Otis Redding, Art Garfunkel and James Taylor. It's also on the movie soundtrack of *Animal House*, *Witness*, and *Hitch*. That song, Adler said, has been "very, very good [to me, and] good to my kids."

Cooke died in 1964, the victim of a shooting in Los Angeles. By that time, Adler and Alpert had already left Keen. Kim Fowley (who would later form The Runaways with Joan Jett) suggested to his University High classmate Jan Berry (of Jan and Dean) to call Adler. Adler and Alpert wrote the duo's first hit, "Baby Talk," and then became their managers as they created the "surf music" sound that came to signify Southern California the world over, with hits such as "Surf City" (written by Brian Wilson), "Dead Man's Curve," and "Little Old Lady From Pasadena," among others.

Berry liked to play volleyball after school at Will Rogers State Beach, and Adler began hanging out there, too, designating the public phone booth as "his office" and instructing anyone who picked up the phone to answer it as "Herb B. Lou Productions."

By 1965, Adler had started Dunhill Records (Alpert had moved on to pursue a performing career, to great success with the Tijuana Brass; he later founded A&M Records with Jerry Moss). At Dunhill, Adler produced a string of hits that also came to define California and the 1960s with Barry McGuire's "Eve of Destruction (a P. F. Sloan song Adler brought to McGuire) and Scott McKenzie's "San Francisco (Be Sure to Wear Flowers in Your Hair)," which would become the anthem of the hippie flower-power movement worldwide.

For his part, McGuire invited his friend Cass Elliot and her friends John and Michelle Phillips and Denny Doherty to visit him during a recording session and to audition for Adler. They were ushered into a small studio where Adler watched as they sang four or five songs, including "California Dreamin'."

"It must have been the same feeling that George Martin had when he first heard the Beatles," Adler said. "This was something so special, something not in rock 'n' roll." Adler envisioned something even greater, Michelle Phillips has said, than even they saw in themselves, and she believes only Adler had that kind of vision. He listened with his eyes closed: "Hearing these amazing voices and lyrics," he remembered, he was struck, when he opened his eyes, by how they didn't look like anyone else in the business. "They were coming off sixty or seventy acid trips, and they were funky…Cass was as big as anyone you'd ever seen, and Michelle was as beautiful as anyone you'd ever seen."

Adler saw this contradiction was worth promoting, and he went so far as to title their first album "If You Can Believe Your Eyes and Ears," which spun off not only "California Dreamin'," but also "Monday, Monday."

During the summer of 1967, John Phillips and Adler produced the now-legendary three-day Monterey Pop Festival, which featured many artists not well-known in the United States and who certainly had never seen one another perform. On the lineup were Janis Joplin, Jimi Hendrix (introduced by Brian Jones), The Who, Laura Nyro, Otis Redding, the Grateful Dead, Buffalo Springfield, Jefferson Airplane and Ravi Shankar, among others, playing to an outdoor audience of as many as 90,000 people.

Also there were many music industry executives, among them Joe Smith and Clive Davis. For everyone, Monterey Pop was a revelation, and not only because of the talent. For the first time, press came from all over the world to cover the American music scene (as opposed to the Beatles and the Rolling Stones). Afterward, in many ways, the music business was never the same. FM radio's focus on album-oriented-rock began to extend the artists' reach, and artists became more influential over their own careers, starting to demand greater control of their music and the cover art on their albums.

The music business was no longer about three-minute radio hits. They discovered, Adler said, "that an artist can not only have a hit, but can have a catalog and a legacy."

Rock 'n' roll became big business.

That same year, Adler sold Dunhill Records. He had never meant to have a label so big that he wasn't personally involved with all the artists, managing them and personally producing their records.

Case in point: In the early 1960s, Adler spent time in New York looking for songs for his artists. Through the impresario Don Kirshner, he met Gerry Goffin and Carole King, and got to know King well. In 1969, when she moved to Los Angeles, she looked up Adler. He produced her first solo album, "Writer," in 1970; it broke the Billboard 100. Yet, well-known as a songwriter, she was reluctant to tour and perform. So for her next solo album, Adler decided that rather than make an album to tour, her songs should sound like they did when she played them for herself and for him.

Adler said King liked to make demos that were "mostly vocal and piano and overdub piano." Adler wanted to capture the intimacy of King playing and singing to the listener, and the result was the "Tapestry" album, which won four Grammys, including Record of the Year, and is still one of the best-selling albums of all time.

Adler's incredible run of luck continued in the 1970s: "I just kind of kept my eyes and ears open. Either I ran into them, or they came to me, or somebody said to me, like they did with *Cheech and Chong*, 'You should go hear them at the Troubadour.'"

Not everyone could see the comedy duo's potential. As Adler recounted in his Hall of Fame acceptance speech, when he first saw them at the Troubadour, "They were on all fours crawling around the stage, sniffing each other's butts." Yet this same duo recorded one of the most successful comedy albums of the era, and they ushered in a new generation of rock 'n' roll comics. The duo's movie potential was also not immediately evident—it took seven or eight years to get a movie deal at Paramount, and then the director dropped out. Adler continues: "Paramount said, 'You know the material. Did you ever think about directing?' I said, 'No, but I'll try it.'"

Count that as one more success story for Adler: "I liked it a lot. Even in the recording [industry], I enjoyed the mixing of the album, where it's just me and an engineer in the studio. In making films, you're dealing with hundreds of people and a crew, but, eventually, it's you and an editor and that part of it I liked it a lot. The experience on 'Up in Smoke' was great. I really enjoyed it." The film went on to become the highest-grossing comedy of the year.

In 1973, Adler opened the Roxy Theatre on Sunset Boulevard; his original partners were David Geffen, Elliot Roberts, Peter Asher and Elmer Valentine. Neil Young played the first week; Peter Gabriel and Genesis a few months later; and the whole gamut—from Frank Zappa, Van Morrison, and George Benson, to Joan Jett, Warren Zevon, Jane's Addiction, Sum 41, and Ariana Grande have performed and recorded there. Adler also had interests in the Whisky a Go Go and the Rainbow Bar & Grill.

The year 1973 was also when Adler's first son, Nikolaj, was born, to actress Britt Ekland, who was then living in London. Adler began spending more time there, and Ekland told him to check out a musical, *The Rocky Horror Show*. Shortly afterward, he met one of the show's original producers, Michael White, at a party in London. Adler made a deal then and there for the rights. In 1975, he produced *The Rocky Horror Picture Show*, a film that continues to play the midnight show at movie theaters nationwide to this day and is considered the longest-running release in history.

There is, however, one other artist whose career Adler championed, but who never met with the success of the others: Merry Clayton. She is one of the backup singers featured in *20 Feet From Stardom*. Adler produced three Clayton albums, but her career as a solo artist never took off. To this day, Adler is mystified as to why. "I think we did everything possible to try and break Merry as an artist," he said. "It was the time when there were so many background singers who could have been stars, or should have been stars—Darlene Love, for example. The only one doing what they were doing was Aretha. Maybe she filled the space? Maybe they compared those people to Aretha, [and] they said, 'We have Aretha.' I could never figure it out."

Adler also directed one more movie, "Ladies and Gentlemen, the Fabulous Stains," a little-seen film released in 1982 that featured Diane Lane and Laura Dern. After that, Adler's credits just seemed to drop off. He didn't disappear: He was still seen out and about, increasingly with Jack Nicholson, whom he first met in the early 1970s, and with whom he bought those enviable ringside season tickets to the Lakers.

It would be easy to cast Adler as someone whose time passed and who just faded away. For one, by the late 1970s, music had changed. "Disco came in, [and] I wasn't interested in that," he said. It is also true that Adler had reached a point where he didn't have to work. As he explained: "I made an enormous amount of money in the record business as a result of owning so much of what I was doing...I owned all those albums and continued to own my catalog. I made some good investments. I don't have another business. I bought a lot of property. It just worked out."

His priorities had changed, too. "At that point, I had two kids—Nicolaj, born in 1973, and Cisco, born in 1978 [with Phyllis Somer]. I hadn't spent a lot of time with them. I was always recording. I decided to be a father at that point. Even though I might be up all night, I would get up in the morning to go to a soccer game."

During the 1980s, Adler remained "very single during those times, probably a little wild." He also fathered another son, Sonny, who lives in Denmark. Yet, as Adler admits, despite his accomplishments, his financial success, and the benefits of owning a club on the Sunset Strip, something was still missing.

One night at a Lakers game, he ran into Page Hannah, a TV and film actress he had met in New York through her older sister, actress Daryl Hannah. He invited her to an after-party at On the Rox (the private club above the Roxy), and they've been together ever since. They married in 1992 and have four sons—Manny, Ike, Pablo, and Oscar.

"I've spent a lot of time with the kids. [If I seem] invisible in the music business, I'm very visible in their lives — spending more time with them than most fathers have the opportunity," Adler said.

Through Page, Adler also got involved in philanthropy. Together with actor Paul Newman, they founded The Painted Turtle in 1999 as a West Coast Hole in the Wall Gang camp experience for children with serious medical conditions. Located near Lake Elizabeth in Lake Hughes, Calif., the camp is a place where children get "to celebrate just being kids" with rope courses, horseback riding, zip lines, fishing, and boating. Adler describes it as a "state-of-the-art facility," with which he is still involved.

The Painted Turtle has also provided Adler a new way to remain in touch with the entertainment industry: Each year he produces a benefit event for the charity. Last year's, for example, was a celebration of the music of Carole King featuring performances by Katy Perry, John Legend and Alicia Keys, among many others, hosted by Nicholson, Danny DeVito and Herb and Lani Alpert.

"It's become my passion," Adler said, "the real meaning of my life," for which he credits Page. "Whatever I was missing, she added to my life."

So, here's what I realized about Adler. He actually is not someone who wants to be in the spotlight. He prefers to work one-on-one to write a song, produce an album or a film, or to sit side-by-side with an artist, recording engineer or film editor. Adler left the music business just as executives and managers were becoming stars with reputations as great or even greater than their artists (think Geffen, Irving Azoff, or Jimmy Iovine). The same was happening in the movie business (think Michael Eisner, Jeffrey Katzenberg and Steven Spielberg).

While Adler appreciates his successes, including the recognition of a Grammy and, especially, of being inducted into the Rock and Roll Hall of Fame, he does not seem interested in the business of being a celebrity. He is very down-to-earth, direct and low-key. He continues to be a soothing, supportive presence, so much so that, although he spoke to me for an hour, I felt like I was telling him my secrets. He has always allowed others to be the star, whether his mother, Josie, the artists who trusted him, his seven sons ("my greatest productions") or his wife, Page.

Which is why, despite all his accomplishments, Adler is best known today as the guy sitting next to the star—Jack Nicholson—at the Lakers' games. And he's cool with that. Very cool.

November 15, 2013

THE PRICE FOR BOB DYLAN GOING ELECTRIC

The guitar stood on a stand in a small conference room in corporate offices in Beverly Hills. A black Fender Stratocaster with a white body plate, a few nicks to its side, it looked simple, basic, uncomplicated.

Yet the story that brings this particular musical instrument to auction at Christies in New York on Dec. 6 has put an estimated value on it of $300,000 to $500,000. Let me venture a prediction: it will sell for $1 million.

The guitar belonged to Bob Dylan. The story goes that he left it on a private plane chartered for him by Albert Grossman, his manager in 1965 (or 1966). Fast forward to 2011, when a young woman, Dawn Peterson, contacted PBS's program, "History Detectives," to ask if they could authenticate an electric guitar she found in the attic of her father, Victor Quinto, a private pilot who died in 1971. Her claim was that Dylan left the guitar on board his plane, that at the time Quinto had contacted Dylan's management to ask if they wanted its return—that they had said not to bother—that they would get Dylan another guitar. And so the guitar stayed in her family until she uncovered it, and she wondered if indeed it once belonged to Dylan and what it was worth.

Suffice to say that Grossman is dead, and Dylan and his family never knew, or else never heard of this offer to return the guitar. The guitar was housed in a traveling case that had clearly stamped on it, "Property of Ashes and Sand, Inc.," which was Dylan's production company at the time. Inside was the guitar strap and several handwritten and typewritten song manuscripts. Perhaps others would have made more effort to return what was clearly not theirs. However, as a legal matter, regardless of how the guitar ended up in her possession, under what are invariably referred to as "finder's keepers" statutes, it now belonged to her.

The "History Detectives" devoted an episode devoted to the guitar in 2012. Andy Babuik of Fab Gear, a guitar expert, examined the guitar's wood finish and the thin lines among the frets and treated them as the fingerprints of the guitar—matching them to photographs of Dylan at recording sessions and performances of that time and concluded that not only was the guitar Dylan's; not only was it used at the recording sessions for "Bringing it All Back Home"; not only was it the guitar used at his Forest Hills, NY performance in August 1965—it was the historic electric guitar that Dylan played at the Newport Folk Festival in the summer of 1965, when Dylan shocked the folk world by "going electric"—certainly one of the most famous musical events of popular music history.

The guitar itself is simple. The story that surrounds it, and the occasions on which it was used, rich. My guess, and it is only a guess, is that Dylan in 1965 and 1966 was not carrying his own guitars anymore and was probably not in charge of getting it on and off planes. However, even if he left the guitar on the plane, he would either have assumed someone else would retrieve it for him, or assumed that it would be easily retrieved. No one at the time ascribed historic importance or value to the guitar. Once it was gone, Dylan, in the words of one of his songs, probably "didn't think twice." At the time Dylan's record company, CBS owned Fender, and, no doubt, they were eager to supply a replacement.

The guitar is being sold with its case stenciled, as mentioned before, with the words "Property of Ashes and Sand, Inc.," and the guitar strap inside. The song manuscripts are being auctioned in separate lots, one of which eventually appeared on "Blonde on Blonde," and others appeared on "Biography" and were authenticated by Jeff Gold, a Dylan expert and collector of Dylan autographic material. Christies also engaged these same experts and, once assured of the authenticity of the guitar and manuscript, prepared the items for the Dec. 6 New York auction.

For comparison's sake, one of the highest amounts ever paid for an electric guitar at auction is $959,000 for "Blackie," Eric Clapton's favorite fender Stratocaster, used on "Layla," which he sold to benefit his Crossroads Centre, a drug and alcohol rehabilitation facility in the Caribbean. I'd be surprised if Dylan's guitar goes for less.

Still, if it were up to me, I'd return the guitar to Dylan. That would be the right thing to do. It's his, simple as that.

That being said, I'm not one to begrudge anyone else getting rich by legal means. So here's my somewhat Solomonic solution: Dylan (or one of his representatives) should just buy the guitar back. It's my understanding that in recent years Paul McCartney has been buying up Beatles memorabilia anonymously on eBay and at auction -- because he can and because he prefers to own his own history rather than have others trade on it.

Dylan, I imagine, is less attached to his own things and certainly less attached to his past. Even the film of his 1965 European tour is called "Don't Look Back." So I understand if he has no interest in participating in other's profiting from the sale of what was his. However, that guitar was the sword and the shield that he took into battle, and in the end, he might appreciate his old friend more than the money it would take for its return.

But let's be clear: Dylan going electric would have happened regardless of the guitar, and its significance has everything to do with Dylan and nothing to do with the guitar itself. Yet it is the stories we invest in objects like this simple electric guitar that give a context, an importance and a meaning to these events. And yes, a value to them as well.

November 25, 2013

THE WALLIS: NOW THAT IT'S BUILT, WILL THEY COME?

A giant risk is being taken with The Wallis—as the Wallis Annenberg Center for the Performing Arts in Beverly Hills is being called, and for which the 1934 Beverly Hills Post Office on Santa Monica Boulevard, between Canon and Crescent drives, has been rehabbed to pristine beauty. The former post office building holds a theater school, the 150-seat Lovelace Studio Theater—a multifunction black box theater—and administrative offices, and it is now attached to architect Zoltan Pali's new, cube-like building, which houses the state-of-the-art 500-seat Bram Goldsmith Theater, with lots of underground parking linked to City Hall.

So here's the risk: Now that it's built, will anyone come?

In recent years, Beverly Hills lost the midsized Canon Theatre, nearby Century City lost the grand Shubert Theatre, and eminent bookstores such as Dutton's, Borders, and Rizzoli all have bit the dust. As one literary figure of my acquaintance put it: "In Beverly Hills, shopping, fashion and eating at good restaurants has come to pass for culture." In creating The Wallis, a great deal of money, time, effort, hope and goodwill has been wagered around a few daunting questions: Can a building—and what goes on inside it—change a neighborhood, a city, the spirit of a place? And will audiences be willing to pay for the entertainment and programming that is being booked and planned for this magnificent newly configured space?

The answer, there is reason to believe, is a resounding yes.

I can say this because to ensure success, The Wallis is relying on what, traditionally, has brought success to Hollywood: Hungarians.

That's right. Hungarians. You may think I've been hitting the Tokay too strongly or am hallucinating due to a poppy seed strudel overdose, but no (my tolerance on both counts is exceedingly high). As every schoolchild knows (at least in Budapest), the apocryphal story is that there used to be a sign on a Hollywood movie studio wall that read: "It's not enough to be Hungarian; you have to have talent."

Consider the following: The architect of the renovation and the newly built theater structure is Zoltan Pali, an American-born Los Angeles-raised son of Hungarian refugees, and a partner of the noted architectural firm Studio Pali Fekete (Judi Fekete being his Hungarian-born partner and wife). And what is the first play to launch The Wallis? "Parfumerie"—by none other than Magyar great Miklos Laszlo—which was adapted into the films *Shop Around the Corner* (with Jimmy Stewart directed by Ernst Lubitsch), *In the Good Old Summertime* (with Judy Garland), and *You've Got Mail* (starring Tom Hanks, directed by Nora Ephron); and as the musical *She Loves Me*. So Hungarian insurance abounds. But is that enough?

First, a little history: The Beverly Hills Post Office was built as a Works Progress Administration (WPA) project on the site of a former Pacific Electric Railroad station in 1933. The story goes that Will Rogers wrote a letter to President Roosevelt saying the city had been promised a post office—and upon a commission's investigation, the funds were awarded for it to be built. Its architect was Ralph Flewelling, and Alison & Alison, an architectural firm known for UCLA's Royce Hall and Wilshire Boulevard Temple. The WPA also provided funding for California artist Charles Kassler to paint several murals about the everyday folk who would use the post office, as well as some frescoes on the history and future of the US Postal Service. The building opened in 1934 and served Beverly Hills over the decades as the city's fame grew as a destination for tourists and locals alike. In 1998, the post office was decommissioned, however, and a group of Beverly Hills residents rallied to save the building.

In 2000, the City of Beverly Hills awarded the lease for the post office property to what was then called the Beverly Hills Cultural Center Foundation, at which point they hired Lou Moore, who had worked six years at the Geffen Playhouse, as managing director. Over the next decade, a series of RFPs—request for proposals—went out, architects submitted plans, architects were chosen, architectural plans were considered and rejected, other architects applied, until they decided to get the Hungarians on board.

As Moore told me recently, "At the end of the day, the board [and] the Annenberg Foundation hung in there. We were not going to give up because this was an extraordinary historic building that deserved to be brought back to life for the community." Moore said the project got support from a wide group of donors. "A lot of the people gave gifts in honor of restoring this landmark, or [because of] how important the arts are to their life, [or because] they wanted more accessible arts."

It was Pali, who as a child had often visited the post office, who proposed restoring the post office as well as building a separate structure for the new theater. The post office now serves as the gateway to the complex. With its floors buffed to a high sheen and the murals restored, it is a jewel of a building, perhaps more glorious than it was upon its official dedication in 1936.

It was also Pali who, upon considering the original use of the site where the new theater would reside, considered the following: What if all the envelopes, once opened, with all their contracts, legal notices, love letters, all were to come back to the post office? And so the outside of the new theater is made of cement panels whose forms suggest envelopes with their corners ripped open. However, Pali was careful not to let the new building overshadow the old—he sunk his design so its roof would be lower than the post office's.

"I had come up with the idea early on that I was not going to copy the architectural elements of the old building. We have do something that is of today but is a conversation with the old building, a young guy and an old guy, Miles Davis and Branford Marsalis—they could have a conversation, they could get on stage and play a duet together. I saw it as a duet."

Moore's vision for The Wallis is that it will become a vital town square. "You might come here and see an exhibition during the day, a show at night, you might have a child in our theater school and sit at our cafe, and you could do that all with parking once."

The programming is equally eclectic, with the Martha Graham Dance Company, aforementioned Hungarian chestnut "Parfumerie," as well as Frederica von Stade, Noel Coward plays and programs, Les Ballets Jazz de Montreal, the Jessica Lang Dance company and "Baseball Swing," a musical event presented in conjunction with the national Baseball Hall of Fame.

"We're presenting theater, dance, music and professional children's theater," Moore said, adding: "Our programming is truly for all ages…We are bringing extraordinary companies from around the world here in Beverly Hills."

All that, and Hungarians, too.

November 27, 2013

DANNY SANDERSON IN LA

CELEBRATING FORTY YEARS OF ISRAELI POP MUSIC

If you've been to Israel in the last forty years or heard Israeli popular music, then you probably know Danny Sanderson, who will be performing with his band at the Gindi Auditorium at American Jewish University on Dec. 8. Sanderson was a founding member in 1973 of Kaveret (literally Beehive; also called Poogy), a band often referred to as "the Beatles of Israel." Although Kaveret broke up in 1976, they have reunited successfully on several occasions. Last summer, for their 40th anniversary, they staged what they announced would be their final dates in Israel, and sold more than 150,000 tickets. Sanderson's successor bands, Gazoz and Doda, have released several successful albums and spawned multiple Israeli radio hits. Sanderson also has written several books, performed stand-up comedy and served as a TV host, and he continues to perform with a seven-piece band of young musicians, including the famed Israeli bassist Yotam Ben-Horin of Useless ID, with whom he is touring the United States. In 2005, Sanderson received a lifetime achievement award for his contribution to Israeli music.

He spoke recently from his home in Tel Aviv; this is an edited version of the interview.

Tom Teicholz: Tell me about the band you'll be playing with in Los Angeles.

Danny Sanderson: The band consists of young and extremely talented musicians that have been playing with me for years, some for 15, some for eight years. Every one of them has their own band, and they are all writers and producers and singer-songwriters. It's one of the better bands I've had — the best since Poogy, since Kaveret.

TT: Does playing with them influence you?

DS: Oh, greatly. One of the ways to feel young is to [work with] people who are connected to what's happening. Musically, it's a thrill, and it's challenging at the same time. They give their own twist to what I do. But, basically, it's a give-and-take. We learn from each other.

TT: This summer, you had a very successful Kaveret reunion.

DS: We were celebrating forty years, and it was a wonderful birthday, to the extent that a lot of people showed up for it. It was wonderful to put the band—I don't want to say "to rest," but ...

TT: But Kaveret has come out of retirement on several occasions.

DS: This was truly "the last waltz." We stated it was, and certainly we meant it from an Israeli point of view.

TT: Over the course of your career, you've played a wide variety of musical styles. What will you be featuring in your LA concert?

DS: It will be "the best of…" and totally retrospective. We give the full spectrum of what I've done, whether it's songs from Kaveret, or Dodo, or the other bands I was in, and certainly from my personal career. We really try to give the crème de la crème.

TT: You've also done a fair amount of stand-up comedy.

DS: That's almost a hobby. It's my second love, my first love being, obviously, writing songs and music.

TT: Will you incorporate some of your stand-up in your show?

DS: In the States, sure. We were just in South America—people were less fluent in English, or Hebrew for that matter [so it was difficult]. Here, I have a means of communicating at least. I'll probably do it in Hebrew, but once in a while I'll explain things in English [so that] people who don't know Hebrew will know what's being talked about.

TT: Hebrew may not be the most beautiful spoken language.

DS: There are some difficulties with it being such a guttural language.

TT: But I've always been struck with how well Hebrew works for rock 'n' roll.

DS: To be honest, I've given this much thought. Every time I do write a song, I kind of try to find the easier-sounding words, the ones that would lend themselves better to the melody. In itself, it's a topic that I address quite often in writing a song. The actual sound of the words beyond their meaning.

TT: All the way back to King David, there is something about the Hebrew language that lends itself to song.

DS: Interesting. Israeli music is a melting pot of society. You have a burst of cultures; cultures have come together and burst into a tremendous combination. You have the Slavic, and the Oriental, Greek, Arabic and German—an extraordinary stew. Israeli music can be very interesting.

TT: It's endlessly varied and creative.

DS: Absolutely. I found myself lured—is that the right word?—to Arabic music when I was much younger. Everyone playing without notes or notation, which is similar to rock 'n' roll, and, to make a blues analogy, Oum Kalthoum, the great Egyptian singer, would sing a phrase and the orchestra would answer with a riff.

TT: Call and response!

DS: Yes, like Buddy Guy singing, "Since you left me," and then a guitar riff would follow. Which, although very different music, is still astoundingly similar to the tradition in Arabic music. In fact, we'll be doing a song in the show that is really as close as we get to that form of Arabic music. That's an instrumental number that we did in Kaveret.

TT: Kaveret and your other bands have been so integral to Israeli culture. How do you see Israeli music as having evolved over the last forty years?

DS: It's come truly a long way. It has its own original form. It's very local, but at the same time very appealing for foreigners as well. Guys like Idan Raichel have taken Israeli music into world music.

TT: How is Tel Aviv for music?

DS: Tel Aviv is culturally extremely open. Israelis are great fans of any good music. And the acts that perform here can be from Burt Bacharach to Red Hot Chili Peppers. Everything is very well received. Israelis go out—a lot—and the club scene is now at one of its peaks.

TT: Finally, what can the audiences expect from your L.A. show?

DS: Aside from the wonderful band that I'm with, we give the audience a [great time]. I've been around for quite a few decades, forty-five years of being in the industry, and I enjoy [performing] tremendously. When the audience joins in, and they frequently do, we truly have a great time. So, we're obviously looking forward to [Los Angeles] because when you come to places that you don't come to that often, there's always great excitement—on both sides. Literally, it's like a date. We're going to dress up and look our best for this Los Angeles date.

December 4, 2013

WE ARE ALL INSIDE LLEWYN DAVIS

Inside Llewyn Davis, Joel and Ethan Coen's new film, is the fictional story of one week in the life of a folksinger in Greenwich Village in 1961. The title character, played with total conviction by Oscar Isaac and supplied with credible material by the maven of American music, T-Bone Burnett, is acknowledged to have been inspired, in part—at least as a jumping off point—by the late folkie Dave Van Ronk. Ethan Coen describes Llwyn as "not a sellout, but he's conflicted." Among the other characters is Al Cody (played by Adam Driver), a cowboy-hat-wearing vocalist whose real name turns out to be Arthur Milgram (much as Ramblin' Jack Elliot, was born Elliott Charles Adnopoz to Jewish parents); while John Goodman plays a junkie musical maestro who bears more than a passing resemblance to the late Doc Pomus (born Jerome Solon Felder).

Llewyn performs traditional songs of a morose nature ("Hangman, Hangman" being a prime example), sleeps on friends' couches until he quickly wears out his welcome, discovers he may have impregnated a friend's wife and arranges for her abortion even as he discovers that another woman he'd gotten pregnant two years before had his child but never told him. He makes one bad choice after another, refusing royalties on a novelty song that takes off, traveling to Chicago to audition for an impresario who rejects him, almost visiting his child, who lives in Akron, Ohio, but doesn't.

Llewyn disdains the inauthentic, the square world, the sellouts, but he still longs for success. He even lacks enough funds to rejoin the Merchant Marine to ship off when he decides to quit the music scene. When he drinks, he becomes belligerent and insults a singer, earning himself a beating from her husband—meanwhile, another folksinger takes the stage at the their favorite stage, the Gaslight, for a performance that will make his career.

In other words: it's a typical Coen Brothers movie about missed opportunities, bad luck and losers who can't help themselves.

Recently, when I sat down with the Brothers Coen in Beverly Hills amidst the "Llewyn Davis," to ask why they'd chosen to tell Lewyn's story rather than, say, a Dylan-like figure, i.e., a first-rate artist surrounded by lesser talents. Both Coens seemed genuinely surprised by the question—"It would just never occur to us," Ethan said.

Joel added that it was not something they had ever, even remotely considered. Never having thought about it before, Joel surmised that "it might have something to do with [the fact that] there's no drama that's interesting to us in triumph over adversity, or emerging success—unless, of course, it's followed by horrible failure. Unless it's the prelude to something else, it seems so un-dramatic and uninteresting."

Their work is the evidence. From the comic in *Fargo* and *Raising Arizona*, to the glorious in *The Big Lebowski*, the manic in *Barton Fink*, and the splendid in *O Brother, Where Art Thou?*, to *The Hudsucker Proxy*, *The Man who Wasn't There*, and *A Serious Man*, all offer an inventory of failed ambitions and of lives filled with waiting for a stroke of luck that never comes. It would be hard to cite other filmmakers whose protagonists fail so often—or so well—over the course of almost two dozen films.

All of which made me think: Are we not all Llewyn Davis? Who among us is not in some way a failure? None of us cheat death. None of us entirely avoid disappointment, illness, loss. Even for the most successful, there is a cost to family or self. In the end, are we not all the sum of our bad choices and mistakes?

So I asked the Coens whether they see the world as a collection of failures, or themselves as such, and whether they harbor reservations about their own successful film careers.

The answer: They do not. "We've been very lucky," Ethan said, "We've never had to think about it."

As for what set the Coens on lucky path, let me digress to the anecdote with which I began my conversation with the Coens.

"Let me set the scene," I said somewhat theatrically, "It's 1984. The Deauville American Film Festival, in France. The first time *Blood Simple* (the Coen Brothers' first film) was screened. It was in the afternoon – and the movie still had no American distributor…"

They nodded.

"I was there as a young journalist for *Interview Magazine*, basically, my editor said that if I got there on my own dime, I could cover it. I was there with my friend, Larry "Doc" Karman, the cameraman, who's still shooting and doing steadicam on films—we were travelling on what I called "The Depressed Men's Tour of Europe."

Joel recalled that "no one paid for us to go over there [either]. We had to get a charter flight to Amsterdam and get on a train. All they paid for was our hotel room at the Normandie." Ethan added, "And I had to share my room, platonically, with a friend of ours."

"That was true for us as well," I said. "The festival paid for one room, which Larry and I had to split. And after the screening, where the film was well received, Larry and I started talking to you,, and that night we all went out to dinner along with Frances [McDormand, now Joel's wife]. We had dinner at a restaurant in a bistro on the waterfront of Trouville. And at the end of dinner, Larry and I picked up the check saying, "If the film is successful, then the next one's on you."

"I do vaguely recollect [that]," Joel said.

Ethan's memory was more fuzzy, but he concluded, "You are entitled to collect."

So when Ethan said, "We've been lucky," I countered with: "So you see, one free meal and that set you on your way."

In a very Coen-like fashion, it was a chance encounter at a turning point. The Coens wanted to make movies, and they've been lucky enough to be able do so. Their films' protagonists, Llewyn Davis among them, may be frustrated and challenged, but the Coen brothers, even after thirty years, seemed remarkably unchanged—a bit weathered, but still as open, guileless and thoughtful as they were so long ago over dinner.

For my part, at the time I felt I had some stories to share, as well as some insight into film and literature, as well as artists, writers and directors. And I've been fortunate to get to share those. But then again, I'm still waiting for that free meal...

December 6, 2013

THEO BIKEL PLAYS JEWGRASS

Although I know it will disappoint some readers to learn that "A Jewgrass Revival," at American Jewish University on Feb. 1, will not be a presentation of the latest Israeli hydroponic farming techniques for marijuana, I can say with confidence that this evening of Jewish Bluegrass music featuring Theodore Bikel and hazzan Mike Stein of Temple Aliyah in Woodland Hills will produce feelings of elation and wonder without any attendant paranoia or munchies. No less a source than Bikel himself guarantees, "It'll be fun."

Moreover, it offers an excellent opportunity to celebrate and enjoy Bikel who, at eighty-nine years young , is also a newlywed, having married journalist Aimee Ginsburg on Dec. 29. Asked about his decision to marry at this stage of life, Bikel answered: "I found this most wonderful woman who is in every way my soul mate...I found in her something that I thought I would have to do without for the rest of my days. I was resigned to live out my life as half a person, but it turns out that I didn't have to."

Bikel's wedding followed his return, a few days before, to his native Vienna, where he performed in the Austrian Parliament, having fled the country seventy-five years earlier for the crime of being a Jew.

Bikel, whose Zionist parents named him for Theodore Herzl, recently recalled how much Vienna has meant to him. Vienna was, Bikel said, "where I learned to be a human being—I learned to love literature, theater, art and music. It was also a place that allowed me to develop as a Jew until that fateful day when everything changed." As Bikel recalled, "A young boy of fourteen overnight became an object of derision and of hatred and of persecution and eventually became a refugee—that was me."

The family fled to Palestine in 1938, earning British passports, and there Bikel began his acting career, co-founding the Cameri Theatre. In 1945, he won a place at the Royal Academy of Dramatic Art in London, and, a few years later, Bikel found himself in a West End production of Tennessee Williams' *A Streetcar Named Desire*, appearing with Vivien Leigh in a cast directed by her then-husband, Sir Laurence Olivier. He also had a small part in John Huston's film *The African Queen*, which starred Humphrey Bogart and Katharine Hepburn.

Bikel immigrated to the United States in 1954, becoming a citizen in 1961. He starred in countless one-hour dramas during the golden age of television, including several written by Rod Serling. In 1959, he originated the role of Captain Von Trapp in the Broadway production of *The Sound of Music*, and he appeared as the dialect coach in the film version of *My Fair Lady*. His performance as Tevye in the original

Broadway run of *Fiddler on the Roof* has, according to Wikipedia, led to his performing the role more than 2,000 times during the course of his career.

However, as Bikel looks back at his long history, what matters most to him are those moments "where I can say that a difference was made." Bikel has been a tireless advocate for human rights and for providing forums where others might speak out for their rights. Bikel founded Los Angeles' first folk club, the Unicorn, as well as the club Cosmo Alley, where Lenny Bruce performed and Maya Angelou read her poetry.

In the late 1950s, Bikel released several albums of Jewish folk songs, and, in 1959, he founded the Newport Folk Festival with Pete Seeger, Oscar Brand, George Wein and Albert Grossman. The festival provided the soundtrack for the social justice movements of the 1960s. He also performed at voter registration drives in Greenville, Miss., in 1963, and later that year at the March on Washington.

"People did not draw the parallel between what happened to Jews in Germany and what happened to blacks in the United States," Bikel said. "I drew the parallel immediately. To me, when a person or a group is being disadvantaged because of who they are, what they are or what they believe in, or the color of their skin—immediately in my mind they become Jews."

He has been involved with issues large and small, from the struggle to free Soviet Jewry to serving on the board of Actors' Equity. And throughout it all he has continued to play music.

Stein, who conceived the idea for the Jewgrass concert, first met Bikel in the 1990s at a Chicago Jewish festival. Raised in Queens, NY, Stein's first career was on Broadway, where he played Peter in the original Broadway production of *Jesus Christ*

Superstar. Several years later, looking for some stability, he auditioned for the United States Navy Band and got a position as a fiddler in one of its bluegrass and country-and-western bands. Shortly after he retired from what became a seventeen-year career in the Navy, he received a call from musical impresario Craig Taubman, whom he had played with, about an opening for a cantor in Woodland Hills.

Stein took the position in 2000. After moving to California, he reconnected with Bikel. "I started getting invited to these music soirées—and he [Bikel] got to know my family; my sons are all musicians and my wife is a singer. I invited Theo over to my house for a jam session with a bunch of bluegrass guys, and he had the greatest time." So, Stein thought: "Why don't we get some of my bluegrass guys and do a gig with him? That's how it came into being."

The Feb. 1 concert will be the first time Bikel and Stein have performed together in public. Bikel will play many songs from his folk music days. Stein will perform a bluegrass version of Friday night Shabbat services, concluding with a Yiddish song set to a country beat, during which Stein's sons, Jared and Justin, and Bikel will all join in. Cathy Fink will play banjo and fiddle and Marcy Marxner will play mandolin.

Performing his folk tunes and bluegrass music brings Bikel full circle, much like his recent return to Austria. In Vienna, Bikel sang for ninety minutes, mostly in Yiddish, and addressed the audience in German. "I ended with the anthem of the survivors, 'Never say you are walking the last road' (Zog Nit keynmol). I told them that this song is sung and listened to while standing, and they all stood.

"Seventy-five years later in Vienna at the Parliament," Bikel said, with no small amount of satisfaction, "I could make a statement—saying that the murderers, the mass murderers, the criminals are gone and I'm still here, singing a song of freedom and of peace."

Long may he sing his song!

January 29, 2014

THE STRENGTH OF MA'ALEH FILM SCHOOL

A black-and-white film shows a trial being called to session. In less than a second, it's obvious this is the trial of Adolf Eichmann, in Jerusalem in April 1961, with Eichmann in the bulletproof glass booth. We watch as a witness takes the stand.

We pull back now, in color, to a present-day room where a group of teenagers are watching the footage. A man asks them, "What does the Holocaust have to do with you?" A girl, Avigail Lev, says it has nothing to do with her. The man then asks the teens what they know about Eichmann? Nothing. They Google "Eichmann" and find his Wikipedia entry and start to read. So the real film begins.

The Strength To Tell, a documentary directed by Noam Demsky, won Israel Ministry of Culture Best Zionist Film prize of 2013 and will have its West Coast premiere on Feb. 8 at the opening night event of the Ma'aleh Film Festival in Los Angeles. Neta Ariel, director of The Ma'aleh Film School in Jerusalem, and David Siegel, consul general of Israel in Los Angeles, are expected to attend.

The Strength to Tell tells the story of a group of at-risk teenagers in contemporary Jerusalem whose lives are changed by a unique program at the HaMartef Theater, through which they develop a play based on testimonies of several witnesses at the Eichmann trial. In the process, they met with Holocaust survivors to understand why they testified at the trial, and what doing so meant to them.

We never really learn anything about the program—who runs it or who came up with the idea of using the Eichmann trial in this way, or even who selected the teens. Instead, the film focuses on the teens themselves, and their journey. Avigail is an angry young woman, cut off from her family, a bottled-up rage simmering inside her. She is defiant, dismissive. She has no interest, she says, in being "in the Holocaust." She doesn't want to meet the survivors because she's "not interested in 200-year-old people." Why would she explore their past, she says, when she isn't interested in her own.

"I don't want to dig into my past, I only look to my future," she says.

Haim lives with his family, has always been told that he is stupid and a loser, but he has always been fascinated by the Holocaust even though he's not sure he will be able to relate to or understand the survivors' plight.

We feel we are watching with the teens, as the film shares testimony during the trial from survivors such as Avraham Aviel and Yosef Kleinman; and we witness the teenagers meeting those same, now-aged survivors. At first it is the survivors who talk; later, the teenagers ask questions.

Alchemy occurs. In listening and developing a theater piece composed of words, of movement of scenes about the survivors, the teenagers realize a few things, such as that no matter how terrible is your experience, no matter if you are cut off from your parents, family and friends, no matter how horribly people treat you, you can still go on and live, love and be whole. In understanding the survivors' trauma, the teens gain perspective on their own. In hearing why one person found the strength to go on—they, too, see their own responsibility to something larger than themselves.

As Avigail says, suddenly "you see things so much less superficially." And, as Aviel, one of the survivors, says, you learn that in "falling and getting back up—getting back up is the main part." By the film's end, the way the teens hold themselves, the way they walk is totally different: they become grounded, self-confident and no longer hostile to the world at large.

Ma'aleh Film School, housed in a building in an ultra-Orthodox neighborhood just outside the Old City, near downtown Jerusalem, was founded in 1989 for filmmakers and students from traditionally observant backgrounds. Today, the student population and faculty come from all walks of life, religious and secular, and the students make films that confront such difficult religious and political issues as homosexuality in the yeshiva and domestic abuse, as well as experimental films. The school prohibits nudity or extreme violence in the films, but students have rarely felt constrained by this.

Over time, Ma'aleh came to realize that its collection of student films represents a valuable resource, covering a wide variety of Jewish subjects and reflecting the diversity and creativity of Israel. Out of this was born a program to screen Ma'aleh films on college campuses and for communities all over the world. The Ma'aleh Film Festival Los Angeles was born from this idea.

Today, Ma'aleh needs financial support, as well as exposure—more than ever. In an e-mail sent on the morning of Jan. 2 by Ariel, Ma'aleh's director, she told of a fire that broke out on the school's second floor, which houses its offices, destroying all the equipment, records and DVDs, as well as damaging the walls and roof, all of which will have to be replaced.

Which is why she would love as many people as possible to go to Museum of Tolerance on Feb. 8 to view *The Strength to Tell*, a film that speaks to the transformative and healing powers of empathy across generations—and of the importance, as well, of the Ma'aleh Film School in Jerusalem.

February 7, 2014

POLLOCK'S "MURAL": MASTERPIECE OR MACHO OUTBURST?

Rarely do we see singular artworks that, even as they represent an exact moment of transition between art historical movements, are also masterpieces in their own right. Yet that is exactly what can be seen now at the Getty Museum, which, until June 1, is showcasing abstract expressionist painter Jackson Pollock's pivotal, eight-foot-high and twenty-foot-wide "Mural," commissioned in 1943 by the collector and patron Peggy Guggenheim for her New York home.

The Getty's conservators have spent the past two years repairing the work for its owner, The University of Iowa, and before its return home, the Getty is presenting a tightly focused exhibition centered around the work, co-organized by the Getty Conservation Institute (GCI)'s senior scientist Tom Learner and the Getty Museum's senior conservator of paintings Yvonne Szafran. The exhibition features one gallery showcasing the mural, surrounded by the facts of its creation, and a second gallery devoted to the conservation project and all that the conservators uncovered about the work's storied creation.

"Mural" is beautifully composed, and contains its own internal logic and rhythm. Yet, unlike Pollock's famous drip paintings that would follow, in this work the artist is still exploring his fascination with often amoeba-like anthropomorphic forms, all revealing Pollock's signature confidence and personality.

"Mural" is notable in several respects. In 1943, Pollock was little-known, so Guggenheim's commission for such an enormous work inspired the largest painting Pollack had done yet—so grand that he had to remove a wall in his home studio to paint it. The Getty analysis reveals that it was an important transitional work for the artist, in that he painted it vertically, rather than laying the canvas on the floor, as he would do with later works. He also, for the most part, used premium, high-quality paints and worked with brushes on most of the work, rather than dripping his paint or using other implements.

However, as would later distinguish his work, Pollock also used some house paint, and in some spots, he flung paint to achieve certain effects, a sign of his method that would follow. This painting, therefore, is the critical bridge between Pollock's more traditional work and the action painting that would distinguish him as among the greatest artists of the 20th century.

It is worth pausing here for a second to acknowledge the importance of Pollock's patron. Guggenheim was born in 1898, into a wealthy German-Jewish "Our Crowd" family—her mother, Florence, was a Seligman, and her father, Benjamin, inherited a copper-mining fortune and died with the sinking of the Titanic, having changed into evening dress with his valet and vowed to "go down as a gentleman," after placing his mistress and her maid in a lifeboat.

At nineteen, Guggenheim inherited $2.5 million, and in the

1920s she moved to Paris, where she became an art collector and opened a gallery in London. However, as the Nazis were about to enter Paris, she fled to the south of France and eventually to New York, where, in 1941, she opened a combination museum and gallery of contemporary art, called the Art of This Century. Her collection, assembled in Europe, included works by Picasso, Magritte, Man Ray, Dali, Klee and several by Max Ernst, whom she married in 1941 (and divorced in 1946).

When Guggenheim was first introduced to Pollock by one of her assistants, Howard Putzel, Pollock was working as a carpenter. In July 1943, she signed the unknown artist to a year's stipend and commissioned the mural. She did not tell him what to paint, only gave him the freedom to do so.

Pollock's "Mural" was a tremendous success and did much to launch the career of the young painter. Guggenheim, for her part, did not take as well to New York. In 1947, after the end of World War II, she closed her New York gallery and returned to Europe, settling in Venice, where she lived until her death in 1979 and where her palazzo and art collection remain as a museum.

When Guggenheim left New York, the Pollock was too large to transport, so she loaned it to Yale University and eventually donated it to The University of Iowa. Moving a painting of such scale—from Pollock's studio to Guggenheim's home, from there to be photographed, then to Yale and to Iowa—inevitably caused some damage, particularly as the work was rolled up each time it was transported. In 1972, in an effort to preserve the paint, the work was varnished and a backing was adhered to the canvas. Although this saved the composition, there was a cost: The varnish dulled the colors, while the backing perpetuated sag that had developed in the canvas.

By 2009, the painting had decayed further, and experts from the Getty were invited to Iowa to assess the damage. Although the Getty's painting collection does not extend beyond the 19th century, the GCI has been conducting a scientific study of modern paint materials for many years and was eager to apply what they have learned to Pollock's "Mural."

Their examination led to some important finds:

The Getty's research debunks some of the long-held myths about the work. In an account in Guggenheim's autobiography, as well as in one by Lee Krasner (Pollock's girlfriend when he painted the work, and later his wife), when Pollock received the commission from Guggenheim in June 1943, she told him she wanted the painting ready for a New Year's Eve party she was having in her Manhattan townhouse, and she told him the painting should take up an entire wall in her entryway.

The story was that Pollock was stymied by the enormity of the commission, but then, on the night before his deadline, in an alcohol-fueled frenzy, he began and completed the work. The Getty's research found this only partially true. The analysis of the paint and its layers revealed that a large part of the painting was painted in one sitting. However, beneath the surface were several layers of oil paints, which dry slowly, proving that the painting was completed not just overnight, but over time.

Accordingly, whereas the work was previously thought to have been painted in December 1943, it is now dated between July 1943 and Jan. 1, 1944. Rather than being the product of a drunken, macho explosion, it's now clear that Pollock made considered choices about the quality of his paints and the multitude of colors (as many as twenty-six were used in the painting), and he employed a variety of brushstrokes and effects to produce the final result.

"Mural," therefore, is a complex, painterly creation that was totally original and that no one could dismiss as mere decoration. Now that years of accumulated grime and dust has been cleaned off, the varnish removed and the painting restretched on specially designed stretchers—we can once again see what Peggy Guggenheim's guests first saw: A rough-hewn poetry of motion, as well as a painter's career in evolution at its most critical moment.

April 2, 2014

SANFORD "SANDY" FRANK: AN APPRECIATION

Sanford Jay Frank, the Emmy Award-winning writer and producer, screenwriting guru and conservative ideologue whom everyone called Sandy, died at his home in Calabasas on April 18 of complications arising out of a glioblastoma, a cancerous brain tumor. He was fifty-nine.

Frank grew up in Springfield, Mass., where his father worked at the post office. He attended Harvard, where he found an outlet for his humor when he joined the Harvard Lampoon, also creating lifelong friendships with Jim Downey (*Saturday Night Live*) and Lawrence O'Donnell (*The Last Word With Lawrence O'Donnell*). Frank graduated from Harvard Law School and became an associate at the prestigious law firm Donovan Leisure.

However, as Frank told the Chicago Tribune in a 1985 article, "There wasn't room for humor in a law firm." So he took what would turn out to be a better-paying job, writing for *Late Night with David Letterman*. The hardest part of the job, Frank said, was learning to stop dressing up for work.

At *Letterman*, Frank created the legendary 1984 Velcro suit stunt, in which the late-night host donned a suit made of Velcro, jumped on a mini trampoline and adhered to a wall. It became one of the defining icons of Letterman's show and his humor. Frank won four Emmy awards for his writing.

Frank was also on the writing team of the culture-defining sketch comedy show *In Living Color*, which brought prominence to the Wayans family, as well as to actors Jim Carrey, Jamie Foxx and Alexandra Wentworth, and to Jennifer Lopez and Rosie Perez as dancers and choreographers. Frank's recurring sketch "Men on Film" has often been cited as one of the show's most memorable highlights and was a frequent contender for feature film development.

After *In Living Color*, Frank worked on a number of African-American-led sitcoms, including *Martin* and *The Jamie Foxx Show*. What Frank loved about working on those shows, he often said, was that there always came a moment when the performers and writing staff would forget he was a white Jewish kid, drop all their inhibitions and enter a zone where anyone could say what they really felt about the issues of the day—which at the time included the O. J. Simpson trial.

At Harvard, Frank was part of the Reagan-era embrace by young intellectuals of conservative thought that led to the birth of the neoconservative movement led by such Jewish Republicans as Franks' Harvard classmates Eric Breindel and William Kristol, among others. Frank liked nothing more than to take a liberal point of view to its most absurd endpoint in order to deflate it.

The opportunity for Frank to do so in writing first came during Lawrence O'Donnell's short-lived one-hour drama about a freshman senator, "Mister Sterling"; then for a half-hour program that mocked the liberal news media and establishment, *The 1/2 Hour News Hour,* which was conceived by Joel Surnow (*24*) as a conservative answer to *The Daily Show.* It was put on the air by Roger Ailes of Fox News, with Frank as head writer and Dennis Miller, Rush Limbaugh and Ann Coulter as commentators. Although the show never found its footing and was canceled after fifteen episodes, Frank earned the respect and friendship of such conservative luminaries as Coulter and Limbaugh as well as Andrew Breitbart.

Following the show's cancellation, Frank worked on a variety of entrepreneurial and creative projects including founding an SAT and test prep school, and writing what some call the Gemara of screenwriting, *The Inner Game of Screenwriting* (Michael Wiese, 2011). He was also working on a screenplay, which remained unfinished at the time of his death.

Frank battled brain cancer for two years, during which, despite challenging moments, he was able to spend memorably good times with his wife, Pam, and daughters Priscilla (a UC Berkeley graduate who is now the arts and culture editor of *The Huffington Post*), Harley (about to graduate from Berkeley) and Michaela (a freshman at Tulane University). He is also survived by his brother, Eric Frank.

He will be missed by all who enjoyed his comedy, and mourned by all who knew him. May his memory be a blessing.

April 23, 2014

JUDY FISKIN: THE HAMMER'S SUMMER BLOCKBUSTER

In keeping with summer being the season for superhero sequels, the Hammer Museum is presenting "Made in LA 2014," its second biennial selection of contemporary artists working in Los Angeles. Organized by the museum's chief curator, Connie Butler, along with independent curator Michael Ned Holte, the exhibition features a diverse and eclectic mix of thirty-five artists working in a variety of media, and it aspires to be, as Holte told me recently, "The most accurate representation of what's happening in Los Angeles at this time."

Among the works included is *I'll Remember Mama*, a ten-minute film by Judy Fiskin, a well-known artist in her late sixties, known originally for her photography but who turned to film and video fifteen years ago. Fiskin's work has been shown at the Getty, the Museum of Contemporary Art, New York's Museum of Modern Art and The Centre Pompidou in Paris, and I wager you will find Fiskin's *Mama* more enjoyable and more interesting than *Spider-Man 2* and scarier than *Godzilla*.

Fiskin, who I recently interviewed in her LA home not far from the Westside Pavilion, grew up on the Westside of Los Angeles, near Century City—before there was a Century City, when it was still part of 20th Century Fox's studio property. Her father was a stockbroker, her mother a "homemaker" (as they were called then). Her mother, who had been an art history major, was a docent at the Los Angeles County Museum of Art, which was then in the basement of the Museum of Natural History. As a child, Fiskin's mother took her to the county museum, the Getty Villa and the monthly gallery night on La Cienega Boulevard. "My mother was interested in all of it, and she took me to a lot of it," she said.

Fiskin studied art history at Pomona College and then went to UC Berkeley for her master's degree, which she completed at UCLA. "In college, I started reading *Artforum*," Fiskin recalled of the avant-garde art magazine, saying that it was like reading, "the Holy Bible." Through the magazine, she became aware of many artists' work—however, seeing them only as small, two-dimensional photographs heavily influenced Fiskin's aesthetic.

Around 1970, she began to take photographs and develop them herself. "I feel really lucky to have come upon [photography] when that was what you did," Fiskin recalled recently. To work in the darkroom, she said "was so pleasurable."

She said she spent around three years "trying to make some good photographs." However, once she was ready to show the work, she realized that she didn't know anyone in the art world. So Fiskin, twenty-six and, in her own words, "fearless," applied to be co-director of the Womanspace Gallery, a now-legendary artists' cooperative in what was known as the Woman's Building in Los Angeles. There, she not only met artists and made art-world contacts, but she was also in a position to do them favors. Fiskin singles out Judy Chicago as the major force at the time: "Talk about fearless," Fiskin said with admiration. "In my mind, she was the leader."

Still, Fiskin only worked at Womanspace for a year. "It's not that I wasn't a feminist," she said. "I just wasn't their kind of feminist. I wasn't into the rhetoric and the politics.

"My idea was, here is something I want to do. The men own it; so let's go and disrupt it," she added.

Still, in Fiskin's estimation, "Womanspace was very effective. They got press from the moment they opened." And Fiskin is quick to acknowledge that, without the women's movement, she would not have developed as an artist as she did.

Her photographs, which first brought her acclaim, were square small-format images of domestic details, such as flower arrangements and home decorations, compositions that, while referencing more classical artworks, were also depicting the traditional domain of women. There was something sly about Fiskin's early work, a deadpan, wry humor that added layers of meaning to the imagery.

In the mid-1990s, however, Fiskin abandoned photography. "I got sick," she said. "I got an auto-immune disease that runs in the family, and it affected my back and my peripheral joints—my feet. So standing in the darkroom became next to impossible. I could do it for two hours, and then I would be wrecked for several days. And two hours was not enough time, so I was very unproductive," she said.

"And then one day I woke up, and my unconscious mind had given me the idea for a one-minute video, and I said, 'I can do that.' I did that one idea and that was it...Immediately I was on to narrative." Her new medium became film.

"When I first started, I thought that my career was over, and that was OK," she said. "But I did know a lot of people...and the first [video] that I made that I wanted to show in public was 'Diary of a Midlife Crisis.' I took it to Ann Goldstein [a curator] at MOCA, and they showed it for a weekend. For me, that was a huge big deal."

Fiskin took so well to video, in part, because she grew up in LA. "I loved movies, and I grew up in the golden era of the 1960s and seventies. There used to be a film festival here called Filmex," the precursor to the American Film Institute's international film festival and to the American Cinematheque, "and the Z Channel was a huge education, and before the Z Channel, there was the Friday night 'Midnight Movies' on TV—I always watched that."

Over the last fifteen years, Fiskin continued to make films, many of which contained elements of personal video diary and often exhibited inspired comic touches. Her films include *My Getty Center*, commissioned for the opening of the Getty Center; *50 Ways to Set the Table,* which focused on a table-setting competition at the LA County Fair; *The End of Photography*, Fiskin's ode to the lost pleasures of the darkroom; and *Guided Tour*," which features voices of what appear to be museum docents talking about various works. "All Six Films," a survey exhibition of all Fiskin's films, was shown at Angles Gallery in Culver City in 2011.

Holte, the independent curator, who had been aware of Fiskin's work, saw that show and loved it. "I thought it was really terrific, all of them at once, and thought it was a very substantial body of work. I actually included Judy in a Top 10 end-of-the-year list in *Artforum* magazine," he said.

"There's a personality that is all Judy that really emerges in the films and videos," Holte added. "It's there in the photographs, but after getting to know her film and video, the photographs read differently."

In developing "Made in LA," Holte met with many artists, including Fiskin, who had several projects that she was considering, but Holte felt that "none of them was developing in a focused way." Fiskin recalled, that she, too, thought that none of those projects was going to work. What Fiskin was beginning to think was, "I'm old. I'm going to retire."

Curators Butler and Holte decided to issue a challenge to motivate Fiskin: They told her they wanted to include a new work of hers in the show. It worked. As Fiskin recalled, "Once he [Holte] asked me, the next day I produced a script that was just about my mother. It was all there, I just didn't want to do it."

"I'll Remember Mama" explores Fiskin's complicated relationship with her ninety-three-year-old mother, who lives in an apartment in the Wilshire Corridor. It is penetrating and funny—elements are reminiscent of scenes in Woody Allen's work—and, in the end, it is both mysterious and revealing and has layers of meaning. "This is a kind of hidden thing," Fiskin said, in that it references her earlier photographic series "Portraits of Furniture," divulging how those images were "about my mother."

Holte thought it was important to include Fiskin in the exhibition. "There's a level of maturity and confidence in Judy's work, because she knows who she is and has been working so long. Judy's work provides some context to the other work in the show, while, at the same time, sitting comfortably next to it."

For her part, having made "I'll Remember Mama," Fiskin feels re-energized and is already contemplating her next project. "I have an idea for a new film that's so good, I'm not going to tell you," she said, laughing.

Holte is pleased. "I think a show like this can also be just as important and meaningful for an artist like Judy, who's shown at the top museums," he said. "A show like 'Made in LA' can still propel an artist like Judy to make dynamic new work, and that's very exciting."

Speaking of exciting, the best superhero movies all feature an origin story, a form of Oedipal conflict, a towering creature that must be understood to be defeated, and a happy ending. If all this can be accomplished with some tips of the hat to film history, and a few doses of irony, all the better—which is not a bad description of *I'll Remember Mama*, and is why Fiskin's work, and "Made in LA 2014," are worth seeing this summer.

May 28, 2014

JEWISH HEROES OF THE GREAT PATRIOTIC WAR

At the University of Southern California (USC), in the lobby of the Doheny Library, a giant story of Jewish history has been writ large in a small exhibition titled "Lives of the Great Patriotic War: The Untold Story of Soviet Jewish Soldiers in the Red Army during WWII." On display through July, it contains just ten kiosks, including two multimedia displays with snippets of a new video archive.

In Russia and throughout the former Soviet Union, World War II is referred to as "The Great Patriotic War." More than thirty million Soviet citizens served in the war, and more than eightmillion died. Soviet casualties from the war have been estimated at more than twenty-six million, a deep wound in the Soviet national consciousness that touched every family and every citizen.

Until now, little attention has been paid to the 500,000 Jews who fought the Nazis as part of the Red Army, more than 160,000 of whom received medals for their bravery and their service. Until now, the stories of those Soviet-Jewish soldiers have been absent from Holocaust archives, memorial museums, survivor testimonies and historical accounts. This exhibition is part of an effort by the New York-based Blavatnik Archive Foundation to change all that.

Established in 2005, the Blavatnik Archive Foundation was funded by the Blavatnik Family Foundation of Len Blavatnik and his brother Alex, Jews born in Odessa who immigrated to the United States in 1978 and whose successful company, Access Industries, has investments in oil and petrochemicals, as well as media and real estate, including the 2011 purchase of the Warner Music Group.

Julie Chervinsky, director of the Blavatnik Archive, explained in a recent phone interview that the archive includes a collection of Judaica, historical materials, ephemera and posters. Also in the collection are many letters from the front during the war that gave great insight into the personal dramas of Jewish soldiers fighting in Soviet territory—a chapter of Jewish history that, Chervinsky said, "had not been captured at all." Collecting the testimonies of Soviet-Jewish participants in World War II became the archive's mission and its priority. Although by the time its research began, many of the survivors had died or were quite old, yet more than 1,100 survivors currently living in eleven countries have been interviewed. This exhibition is assembled from those testimonies.

Organized both thematically and chronologically, the exhibition describes each phase of the war in both English and Russian texts, through personal photos of the survivors (then and now), as well as propaganda posters and postcards. It tells of the role of Jews in the first Soviet generation, who were also witnesses to and participants in the Russian Revolution. It shows how they felt on the eve of the war against the Germans, and how Russia stoked fear with propaganda films, such as the 1938 "Professor Mamlock," which is one of the first films to address Nazi anti-Semitism. Boris Tsalik speaks of his "love of the motherland," which led him to volunteer for the Red Army. Abram Byakher recalls that the longest day of 1941 was June 22, the night of his high-school prom—and the night Germany invaded Russia.

Hitler's "Operation Barbarossa," the invasion of Russia, was very successful at first. By mid-July 1941, the Germans had moved more than 200 miles inside Russia, and some 4 million Soviets had been captured or killed. It was then that the Soviets made a strategic decision, as shown here, to evacuate, forcing a retreat by some 16 million Soviet citizens. As the Germans advanced farther and farther away from their supply lines, only to find little to no resources on the ground, they became overextended, leaving an opening for the Soviet counteroffensive to launch.

At Stalingrad, Soviets were ordered to cede "not a step back!" Under Stalin's orders, the Red Army used its infantry and tank units to turn the tide of the war. The exhibition features Alexandra Bochalova, Igor Blinchik and Ida Ferrer, some of the Soviet Jews who fought there. According to the Blavatnik Archive, another 20,000 to 30,000 Jewish partisans also fought the Nazis on Soviet soil, helping to liberate Russian territory, as well as Poland, Hungary and eventually fighting all the way to Berlin.

Mark Altshuller was among the Soviet troops who liberated the Majdanek concentration camp. He recalls seeing barracks full of children's hair, shoes and other belongings, the corpses barely incinerated. The sight filled the troops with such rage, they began to execute the remaining German officers on the spot and continued to do so until Stalin ordered them to stop.

There is something both heroic and tragic about the Jewish experience in the Soviet Union. For many Jews in that first generation of revolutionaries, the Soviet Union not only afforded greater rights and the social mobility to leave the shtetls and ghettos of provincial life, it also offered opportunities for education and to pursue professions previously denied to Jews. In return, however, those Soviet Jews had to give up religious observance; being Jewish became merely an ethnic nationality. Then, under Stalin, Jews became doubly cursed: They could not practice their religion, and being identified as Jewish on official documents nevertheless led to discrimination and distrust.

It is heartbreaking to read of Jews who fought at Stalingrad and yet whose hope of a transformed Russia were dashed when they returned home to find their patriotism doubted, their homes and possessions looted, and anti-Semitism officially sanctioned.

I know this truth firsthand from my relative Michael Sherwood, born Meyer ("Misha") Teichholz in Tarnopol, in what was then Poland, who lived this history. When the Germans invaded, he fled to the Soviet Union, and though he was just a teenager, he joined the Red Army and served at Stalingrad. Then he was arrested and sent to the gulag (which probably saved his life) simply for the crime of being a Jew. In 1947, the Soviet officials repealed their decision and released him. He made his way back to Poland, where the Jewish population had been liquidated. He emigrated to Israel, and then to New York, where he lives today. He calls himself a "double survivor," having survived the Holocaust and the gulag—but because he fled to Russia, he was not considered a Holocaust survivor by the European Holocaust organizations; and the United States' organizations looked askance at the fact that he'd served in the Red Army before being falsely imprisoned in the gulag. A few years ago, I was able to help him publish his story, "Odyssey," which is available in print versions and as a free e-book download from lulu.com.

Chervinsky told me one of the most gratifying aspects of the Blavatnik Archive's work comes from the survivors' gratitude that "somebody came and listened to them and treated them professionally." In short, what makes this so meaningful, Chervinsky said, is their "response to not being forgotten." Which is why after seeing this exhibition, I put Sherwood in touch with the archive, so that my own relative's knowledge of the Jewish experience during World War II can be expanded to include the experiences of those ignored for so long, those Jewish heroes of "The Great Patriotic War."

June 11, 2014

ISRAELI ARTISTS OF THE IMAGINATION

Rit Raff and Nir Evron at LAXART

Art—both making it and enjoying it—seems a luxury in times of war. Yet the work of two Israeli artists, Orit Raff and Nir Evron, showing at the contemporary art space LAXART through Aug. 23, is not only a worthy distraction from the psychic weight of current events but also a testament to the power of art to transcend national identities, challenge assumptions and transport viewers to landscapes heretofore unimagined.

The exhibition is supported by Artis, a nonprofit that supports Israeli contemporary art and artists, and which organizes trips to Israel for curators and art professionals to meet their Israeli counterparts and visit artists' studios. It was on one such trip that LAXART's director, Lauri Firstenberg, first encountered Raff's and Evron's work.

Raff's LAXART exhibition, "Priming," consists of images of rooms, buildings and architectural details, each inspired by a different novel, ranging from contemporary works such as Donna Tartt's *The Secret History* (a haunting empty attic) to classics such as Gustave Flaubert's *Madame Bovary* (a bedroom with an unmade bed). The images are not literal representations of literary scenes but rather Raff's detailed visualization of the work, which she describes as "a translation."

At first glance, the images appear stark and challenging, like crime-scene photographs that prompt the question, "What happened here?" They are all the more remarkable because they've been created without a camera; each is painstakingly created on a computer—none of the elements are from actual photos—every detail, shadow and fold of a bedspread has been fashioned by Raff to create the verisimilitude of these imagined spaces.

As Raff explained, we live in a world awash in photographic images, where everyone takes photos and posts them—but she wanted to explore "the territory that is uncovered," which she found in fiction. She said her work is a fiction, too—but one that can be "read" as a photograph.

Raff, born in 1970, grew up in Jerusalem in a family that supported her interest in arts and culture. She took art classes and danced, but only became serious about being an artist when she attended Bezalel Academy of Arts and Design in Jerusalem. Despite it being "very male-dominated" at the time, Raff said, Bezalel nevertheless gave her a "very good and rigorous understanding of photography." After Bezalel, Raff attended the School of Visual Arts in New York, completed an independent study program at the Whitney Museum, and in 2003 received her master's at Bard College. All in all, she spent a decade in the United States before returning to Israel.

Like "Priming," Raff's prior projects explored issues in photography that reflect her "interest in space and architecture and how the body functions within these spaces." For an earlier exhibition, "Dislocated Land," Raff created abstract images by placing large stickers in rooms, then using high-resolution digital scans to record the accumulation of dust—what Raff called "the traces of life." She then enlarged the scans, creating photograms in the tradition of Man Ray's "Rayographs" and Marcel Duchamp's "Great Glass." For Raff, this is "the most direct way of capturing nature."

Raff said her current exhibition has been influenced by her return to Israel.

"Living in such a conflicted place, makes you think about the narratives that are being told, [and] the narratives not being told," she said.

Narratives that are not being told is also a theme in Evron's work "Endurance," the final film in a trilogy. Each film has an architectural reference and foundation, but explores issues of identity and existence differently.

The first, *Oriental Arch* (2009), was filmed at the Seven Arches Hotel on the Mount of Olives in East Jerusalem and features fixed-camera 16mm film of the hotel as its many workers and few guests move through the hotel's public spaces. *Free Moment* (2011), was filmed at the unfinished summer palace of King Hussein of Jordan, which was abandoned during the 1967 Six-Day War and is now in Israeli territory; the film features long dolly shots that make the abandoned moribund space seem mysterious. Finally, *Endurance* is an abstract, camera-less work, recalling the early abstract films of Hans Richter or the Structuralists. It takes the floor plan of a model home in Rawabi, a planned Palestinian suburban community outside Ramallah, and translates its exact dimensions visually—the rooms are black rectangles whose length corresponds to the time they are shown. *Endurance* is shown on a projector configured to run on a loop.

Evron's work, though abstract and without dialogue, nonetheless provokes questions in viewers that range from the artistic to the political. A recent discussion held by LAXART between Nir and novelist Michael Klein of CalArts to discuss *Endurance* became a freewheeling conversation about politics, capitalism and suburban architecture—all prompted by Evron's work.

Evron was born in Herzliya in 1974, to parents who emigrated from Romania and Poland to then-Palestine in 1947. Evron said he started to take photographs as part of his job as an internal affairs detective in the Israel Defense Force. Later, while accompanying a girlfriend who wanted to apply to Bezalel, he discovered the school's program in photography and applied on the spot—and was accepted shortly thereafter. After Bezalel, he received a master's from the Slade School of Fine Art in London, where he discovered experimental film.

"They had a 16mm editing suite and equipment, and because I was trained as a photographer before the digital revolution I basically only knew how to shoot film, so the transition into moving image was really easy for me," Evron said. "I never made videos; I started immediately to make 16mm films."

Evron returned to Israel in 2005, and has had his work shown internationally, including at the 6th Berlin Biennale (2010), The Maison Européene de la Photographie in Paris (2012) and The International Center for Photography Triennial in New York (2013).

In both Evron's and Raff's work, one can see a rigorous intellectual inquiry, built upon extensive research and planning, and executed in a very deliberate and meticulous fashion. Raff's work is pictorial, while Evron's is abstract. Yet both are invented landscapes, rooted in architecture and reclaimed from existing texts or places in which, as Raff noted, "the imagination creates a reality."

It seems fitting that Israeli artists, born of a nation founded on an idea, whose very language is a revival and reinterpretation of ancient texts more read than spoken, should be engaged in the creative interpretation of spaces bearing meaning. Doing so reminds us, in this most difficult of times, that we, as humans, are endowed by our creator with that most human of qualities: our ability to forge a new reality.

July 30, 2014

THE HOLLYWOOD BLACKLIST
IN EXILE

Stories of the Hollywood blacklist of the 1940s and '50s are, by now, well known. Many books, articles and documentaries exist about the lives of actors, screenwriters and directors who the studios deemed unemployable because of their association—real or alleged—with the Communist Party. Also familiar are the stories of many who "named names" to Congress' House Un-American Activities Committee—such as Ronald Reagan, Elia Kazan and Budd Schulberg, who provided names of people they believed were Communists and, in return, were allowed to continue working for the studios. Equally familiar is the fate of those who refused to testify, some of whom — including Dalton Trumbo and Ring Lardner Jr.—went to jail for contempt of Congress.

There is, however, another chapter in this tale, as showcased in "Hollywood Exiles in Europe," UCLA's Film & Television Archive's film series at the Hammer Museum in Westwood, showing through Aug. 17. The series features films by Jules Dassin, John Berry, Ed Dmytryk, Ben and Norma Barzman,

Joseph Losey, Cy Endfield, and Donald Ogden Stewart. All were writers and directors who went to Europe and continued to work under their own names, advancing their careers sometimes to the point they were considered European artists. (Dmytryk returned from exile in 1950 and after naming names was allowed to resume his Hollywood career.) The series is co-curated by Rebecca Prime, whose *Hollywood Exiles in Europe: The Blacklist and Cold War Film Culture* (Rutgers University Press, 2014) tells the previously untold tale of the lives and influence of these filmmakers.

As Jan-Christopher Horak, director of the UCLA Film & Television Archive, points out on his blog, many of the exiles succeeded by bringing film noir to European-made films and making moral tales for morally ambiguous times. Like generations of immigrants and exiles the world over, not all adapted successfully or in the same manner. The series showcases the divergent reactions as experienced by three Jewish exiles to Europe: director and writer Jules Dassin, and screenwriters Ben and Norma Barzman.

Julius "Jules" Dassin was born in Middletown, Conn., in 1911. He grew up in Harlem, NY and joined the Communist Party in the 1930s, but left in 1939 after Stalin signed a non-aggression pact with Hitler. Dassin was a successful director of Hollywood films including *The Tell-Tale Heart* (1941), *The Canterville Ghost* (1944), *The Naked City* (1948), and *Thieves' Highway* (1949). But in 1950, during the production of Night and the City, Dassin was blacklisted. He moved to France, and it would be five years before he produced another film, *Du Rififi Chez Les Hommes*—also known as *Rififi*—which he directed and co-wrote, adapting the story from a French novel.

Rififi is remarkable in part for its nearly thirty-minute heist scene, filmed with no dialogue or music. It has been described as the ur-heist film, and if you've ever watched a film where someone drops down from the ceiling to evade a security system and purloin a treasure, you've seen the influence of *Rififi*—Dassin himself borrowed the scene nine years later for his action-comedy heist film, *Topkapi*.

At the 1955 Cannes Film Festival, Dassin won the Best Director award for *Rififi*. Cannes was also where he met Melina Mercouri, the Greek actress who he would make world famous in *Never On Sunday* (1960) and who he married in 1966; they remained married until Mercouri's death in 1994. Following her death, Dassin ran the Melina Mercouri Foundation, which lobbied the British Museum to return the classical Greek sculptures known as the Elgin Marbles and helped establish the Acropolis Museum with casts of the Marbles. Until his death in 2008, Dassin remained closely identified with Greece and Greek politics, to the point where many assumed Dassin was Greek. One could say Dassin embraced exile, assimilated and, professionally, never looked back.

By contrast, Ben Barzman never acclimated to Europe. Barzman was born in Toronto, Canada, in 1910 and was a journalist and novelist before coming to Hollywood. Following the Great Depression, he joined the Communist Party. In 1942, while attending a fundraiser at screenwriter and director Robert Rossen's home, he met his future wife, Norma, who was also a journalist-turned-screenwriter. She, too, joined the Communist Party. Ben Barzman gained acclaim with *The Boy with the Green Hair* in 1948. However, the following year, he and Norma left for Europe after Marilyn Monroe tipped them off that a policeman was parked at the end of their street monitoring their comings and goings, and Groucho Marx warned them they were about to be added to the blacklist.

The Barzmans spent time in Paris and then settled in the south of France. Ben Barzman continued to write screenplays but constantly felt the stress of exile. He was at times despondent, and often suspicious that US agents were spying on him and his wife. At the time, many thought he was paranoid but many years later, Ben Barzman discovered that indeed FBI agents in the US Embassy had been tracking them.

In 1960, he reinvented himself with great success as a science fiction writer, most notably with the novel *Out of This World* (also known as *Echo X*). During his exile, Barzman wrote commercial European costume dramas such as *El Cid* (1961) for Sophia Loren (for which he was initially uncredited). However, Barzman finally was able to channel his political passion into an uncredited rewrite of Costa-Gavras' political thriller *Z* (1969).

In the 1970s, the Barzmans returned to the US, and Ben Barzman died in 1989 in Santa Monica. Exile had deprived his screenwriting career of its momentum and hobbled him emotionally.

Finally, there is Norma Barzman, who at ninety, continues to thrive. She appeared at the Hammer on July 25 to kick off the film series. The UCLA Film & Television Archive will host a reception on Sept. 15 to honor Barzman's 94th birthday, featuring a screening of *The Locket*, the 1946 film for which she wrote the screenplay.

Norma Barzman found exile to be, in Hemingway's phrase, "a moveable feast." She befriended Picasso, Yves Montand,

Simone Signoret, and blacklisted artists such as Zero Mostel, Endfield and Losey. It was all oxygen to her, even as the same events seemed to dispirit her husband. In 2003, she published a memoir, *The Red and the Blacklist: The Intimate Memoir of a Hollywood Expatriate* (Nation Books), which captures her optimism and enthusiasm.

Too often the Hollywood blacklist stands for repression and betrayal. "Hollywood Exiles in Europe" deepens our understanding of the varied personal and professional responses of affected artists. The artists in this series chose to create new lives elsewhere, a theme that has been oft repeated in Jewish history. Like the story of so many other exiles, some, like Dassin, assimilated and furthered their art; some, like Ben Barzman, could not; and some, like Norma Barzman, while not adopting their host countries, continued to thrive—for she was, as Plutarch said of Socrates, "not an Athenian or a Greek, but a citizen of the world."

July 30, 2014

MARX BROTHERS MAKE MERRY IN TV COLLECTION

The Shout! Factory release of *The Marx Brothers TV Collection*, an omnibus of the Brothers Marx's post-film career TV appearances, is occasion enough to celebrate once more the irrepressible talents of Groucho, Chico and Harpo Marx.

I suppose there may be some readers who have never heard of the Marx Brothers, but I doubt it. In short, at the beginning of the 20th century, hailing from a German-Jewish family, Minnie Marx set her sons on a show-business career hoping to garner some of the success (and steady employment) of her brother, Al Shean, who performed as part of the comedy team Gallagher and Shean. The core of the brothers' act was Groucho (born Julius), who sang and played guitar; Chico (Leonard), who was an accomplished pianist; and Harpo (Arthur), who couldn't sing and so played a man who could not speak but could play harp, clarinet, piano and harmonica. Brothers Zeppo (Herbert) and Gummo (Milton) also made appearances as singers.

The brothers got their start touring a vaudeville act, based on their personalities and talents, under Groucho's creative direction, while Chico ran the business side. By the Roaring twenties, they were stars on Broadway, with their stage comedies *The Cocoanuts* in 1925 and *Animal Crackers* in 1928.

In Hollywood, they started making movies of their Broadway shows as well as original films, including their highest-grossing work, *Horse Feathers* (1932), and their most critically revered film, *Duck Soup* (1933). While under contract with Paramount, their movies were largely extended pieces of vaudeville and improvisational free-for-alls. When their contract with Paramount expired, producer Irving Thalberg lured them to MGM and insisted they have more structured scripts with a beginning, a low point and a happy ending, including romance as prominently in the story line as comedy. Thalberg came up with the innovation of testing some of the brothers' film comedy bits before live audiences. The result led to the Marx Brothers classics *A Night at the Opera* and *A Day at the Races*, movies Groucho adjudged to be their best. After Thalberg died suddenly during the production of *A Day at the Races*, their remaining MGM films were lesser works. By 1949, after forty years in show business, the brothers retired.

Then along came television, allowing each of the brothers a new medium to conquer—Groucho, most notably as host of the game show *You Bet Your Life*, and, in Chico's case, a way to pay for his gambling debts. (When Chico was once asked how much he had lost gambling, he answered: "Just ask Harpo how much he's earned as an entertainer.")

The three-DVD set, to be released Aug. 12, features segments, programs, guest appearances, commercials and even home movies. There are nuggets throughout, including Chico imitating Harpo, Harpo imitating Groucho, Groucho late in life donning his greasepaint mustache again to sing of Dr. Quackenbush.

Throughout, Harpo and Chico never seem to age, or rather they come to look like the characters they pretended to be as young men. Groucho ages physically, but his force of personality is so strong that he maintained his quick-witted persona even to his last appearance in 1976, a year before his death, at eighty-six.

Who is there today to compare them to? We can look to *Saturday Night Live* for producing talent quick-witted enough to host shows, be it Jimmy Fallon, Seth Myers, or Conan O'Brien. Jon Stewart is clearly descended from Groucho. Perhaps only Steve Martin has combined the brothers' musicality and humor to find success in almost as many mediums, remaining relevant to successive generations. But really, when you watch the Marx Brothers, there is a special magic no one has yet come to equal.

The Marx Brothers hold a special place in my heart. When I was little, my grandmother first took me to see one of their films, and in high school I discovered them all over again. The Marx Brothers have nursed me when I've felt sick, or down, when my energy has flagged. One of the great pleasures of my life was introducing my daughter to their films. The Aero Theatre on Montana Avenue has had a tradition of beginning the New Year with a double feature of Marx Brothers films, and for several years my daughter and I attended, laughing together at the antics of Groucho, Harpo and Chico that never seemed to grow old.

If I try to put my finger on what made me, a child of immigrant Jewish refugees from Europe's nightmare, so relate to the Marx Brothers, it would be that I saw characters full of pride and self-confidence, fueled by humor, who didn't assimilate into the establishment so much as triumph over it. That was a life plan.

Groucho was a shyster, a conman, a flimflam artist, a fast-talking insult comic. He was always working an angle, and he said whatever he thought best worked for the situation — which I believed was how many of my relatives and my parents' friends outwitted the Nazis to survive the Holocaust. Groucho was literate, in love with word play; his speech was littered with foreign words and expressions, sometimes of his own invention—talmudically annotated and punctuated with asides, inside jokes and observations to his audience. This, too, was familiar: When you grow up in a household where nine languages are spoken, none of them grammatically or intelligibly, you get a lot of constant commentary. He was the wise son, a wisenheimer, if you will.

Chico was the wicked son. He was a criminal, crafty if not bright, and the leader of a gang of two (usually joined by Harpo). He was something of ashtarker, an accented foreigner — in this way Chico reminded me of some of the "boys"—actually tough guys—who worked for my father in the Bricha—the underground transport system that helped Jews escape World War II Europe. Although Chico seemed to be of Italian descent—he wore a Tyrolean jacket and hat—that, too, was familiar to me: In fact there are some who claim my mother used to dress me the same way.

As for Harpo: Who doesn't love Harpo? Harpo is the simple son. He plays the harp like an angel and acts like a mischievous child, even while chasing women (literally). He is all id and no ego. Finally, Gummo and Zeppo were the handsome good-hearted guys who got the girl. That, too, was an ambition of mine.

All of which is to say that the Marx Brothers were people we could imagine gathered around our seder table (or, more likely, at lunch at Los Angeles' Hillcrest Country Club, where they regularly commandeered a center table, playing cards with George Burns and Milton Berle and letting Rabbi Magnin kibitz or sit in).

The Marx Brothers TV Collection contains some rarities and oddities, such as Groucho's sole dramatic role as a father who disapproves of his daughter's marriage to a very young Dennis Hopper; and Harpo's sole dramatic non-Harpo role, as the silent witness to a murder.

There are also some wonderful moments when each of the Marx Brothers reprise some of their vaudeville numbers. Groucho, who started out doing a German accent until the first world war made that un-commercial, sings a song about schnitzel and, in what is perhaps my favorite clip, he performs a version of Gallagher and Shean's theme song, with Jackie Gleason's brother in the Gallagher role.

What comes through from the home movies and the appearances is how utterly at ease the Marx Brothers were in the world of entertainment—they performed for so long and were so deft at it that they shone in whatever medium on whatever stage or screen you put them on.

There is still so much pleasure in watching the Marx Brothers perform individually or together, so much intelligence in how they deploy their talent, even casually, even in silly commercials, that just the mere glimmer of any of them sets the endorphins rushing, bringing back the totality of pleasure they have offered up, a world in which, as Groucho once put it, "Humor is reason gone mad."

August 6, 2014

IN RE: ARTIST MIRI CHAIS' MIND

"Re:Mind," a multimedia installation at USC's Fisher Museum of Art, is the first solo show in the United States for Miri Chais, an Israeli-born artist who now lives in Los Angeles. For the show, Chais created and installed a room full of paintings and sculptures, as well as objects that have screens embedded in them, all of it accompanied by music (much of it composed by her fifteen-year-old son) and a looped video displayed on the walls behind and surrounding her works. It is a total environment that Chais explained by saying, "I want to control everything."

Chais describes herself as a "post-Internet" artist, by which she means that she makes work that reflects upon a world where much of our culture is played out on screens, and in which our real-life experiences are affected by what we experience online and on screens in two dimensions. "Re:Mind," Chais said in an interview, "is about different states of mind...and the different things that can influence our mind."

Her work, which is harder to describe than to look at, combines brain scans with images related to technology. So, for example, there are paintings in which a large human skull is outlined over what looks like kudzu-green marshes, with drips of black acrylic paint applied to the canvas as well—the total effect of the juxtaposed imagery makes us question what the artist has in mind—literally. Chais often appropriates images from various science-fiction films such as *The Matrix*, and she incorporates found images and film clips from various public domain archives, then places them into her art in the various formats of paintings, sculpture and digital prints. Chais' work is meant to make us consider whether the reality we see, even the memories and thoughts we have, are machine-influenced, man-made or both.

Selma Holo, the Fisher's director, explained that she was drawn to Chais' work by its complexity: "I tend to run across artists who are very interested in technology; I run across artists who are very interested in spirituality, I run into artists who are very interested in beauty for beauty's sake; I run into artists who are very involved in social commentary, but I rarely run into artists who are mixing it all up in such a way."

USC's Fisher Museum was founded in 1939 and is open to the public with free admission. Situated on campus, the museum is part of the Exposition Park complex of museums, and contains a permanent collection of some 1,800 objects, including works on paper, paintings and sculptures, ranging from the 16th century to the present, including from Elizabeth Holmes Fisher's original bequest, as well as from the Armand Hammer Collection and more recent donations.

Holo explained that as a university museum, its mission is "very involved in and excited about the possibility of breaking down walls between disciplines," characterizing the museum as both "interdisciplinary and trans-displinary." It's also an apt description of the multimedia universe of Chais' art, in which eagles fly and a totem called Golem stands displaying video of both Tony Robbins and Jeff Koons; Chais creates a challenging environment, specific and metaphoric, local and global, that speaks not so much to who Chais is, as to what she thinks.

Chais was born in Ashdod, Israel. She originally pursued a career in advertising, however, in her thirties, she decided she wanted a change and went to Hamidrasha College of Art in Kfar Saba. She worked mostly in painting and photography; the installation she did for her graduation was shown at Beersheba University, where it received a positive review in the Haaretz newspaper, launching her career.

In 2011, Chais moved with her husband and their children to Los Angeles (where her huband is from) and she said she is enjoying being here. She has found LA welcoming and supportive: She has a studio in Inglewood's Beacon Art Center, where she gets to meet other artists and feel part of an artistic community.

Chais has come to appreciate the light in Los Angeles, as well as the intangibles of Hollywood's "dream factory." Given that much of her work is an inquiry into images and the cultural impact online and onscreen, as well as science fiction and science fact, she can think of no better place to be than in Los Angeles and Hollywood—with its image-making industry that also strives to impart meaning to the visual. Chais has found in LA a place "where you have the freedom to interact with so many things that inspire you."

Los Angeles also has affected her work. Prior to moving here, she was interested primarily in the two-dimensional nature of screen-driven lives. LA has inspired her to create in three dimensions, not only by increasing the texture added to her paintings and sculptures, but by now conceiving of her work as creating environments—as she has done for her USC exhibition. To put it another way: An art exhibit about thinking and being in a post-Internet world at a university art museum seems quite apropos."

In conjunction with the exhibit, USC has scheduled several programs, including a conversation between Chais and and Fisher curator Ariadni Liokatis, on Oct. 7 at 7:00 p.m.; and on Oct. 15, Andrew S. Gordon, a professor in USC's Computer Science department, will give a lecture titled "Mind Reading for Robots" on current research into how our mind works. (That one will be presented in collaboration with USC's Israel Initiative for the Arts and Humanities.)

Holo hopes to engage further crosspollination between the faculty and Chais in both student and public forums. "She will have a lot of intellectual backup here, to see how her world resonates in a larger intellectual context," Holo said.

October 1, 2014

LEONARD COHEN'S TRIUMPHANT PROBLEMS

The mere release of *Popular Problems*, two days after Leonard Cohen's 80th birthday last month, is remarkable in and of itself. (How many eighty-year-old sex symbols and style icons are there?) But it also caps a decade in which Cohen conquered troubling neuroses and fears to mount worldwide tours that were invocations, convocations and spiritual gatherings, not to mention money-makers, that returned Cohen, who'd been swindled out of his lifesavings, to financial security. His is one of the more amazing runs in music history.

Nomen est omen. The name determines the life. In Cohen's case, he has become the priest, and not just for a cadre of followers around the world; he is also a seeker, a pilgrim ever struggling to find satori—in wine, drugs, women, in isolation and among the world, in words and in song.

Popular Problems finds Cohen's baritone deepened, his voice more raspy, but each word distinct, each phrase launched like an arrow at a target. The accompaniments, produced by Patrick Leonard, are spare—piano, violin, a chorus of back-up singers, digitalized beats that are melodic in contrast to Cohen's own probing lyrics.

This may be my favorite collection since 1988's *I'm Your Man*. It is about optimism in the face of age, war, terrorism and the ongoing challenges of love. Cohen opens with "Slow," a sly declaration of style over age, singing "It's not because I'm old / It's not the life I led / I always like it slow / That's what my momma said."

"Slow," however, is no oldster's apologia, but rather a credo akin to slow cooking, or slow networking, an acknowledgement that slow and mindful is how to savor life—a feat Cohen has spent a lifetime pursuing.

A decade ago, Cohen was ready to retire. He had become overwhelmed by a fear of disappointing his live audiences that he could not go on stage. Then, after becoming a victim of embezzlement forced him back to work, Cohen took up a tour so arduous—filled with three-hour shows each night—a tour so powerful, so joyous, so satisfying, that in just three years, Cohen earned his way back to financial stability. *Popular Problems* is a capstone to the artist's triumph over his own demons. In "A Street," he sings, "The party's over / But I've landed on my feet / I'll be standing on this corner / where there used to be a street."

The nine songs on *Popular Problems* present meditations on Jewish heritage replete with biblical imagery ("Born in Chains"), and applies that imagery to Hurricane Katrina ("Samson in New Orleans"), love and love lost ("My Oh My," "Did I Ever Love You") and war ("Almost Like the Blues") and songs that combine them all ("Nevermind"), tackled with both seriousness and self-deprecating humor. As he sings in "Almost Like the Blues," "There's torture and there's killing / There's all my bad reviews / The war, the children missing / It's almost like the blues."

One cannot read the lyrics on *Popular Problems* without appreciation for the zen of Cohen: His words are heavy with meaning, with counterpoints of humor, irony or cynicism; there's meter to his lines and, occasionally, a clever rhyme. His lyrics present a man at home with his past and with his cultural tradition. He sings, "My father says I'm chosen / My mother says I'm not / I listened to their story / Of the Gypsies and the Jews / It was good, it wasn't boring / It was almost like the blues." He even ends his album on a declaration of optimism as plain as it is direct, "You Got Me Singing."

"You got me singing / Even tho' the news is bad / You got me singing/ The only song I ever had…You got me thinking / I'd like to carry on."

Rave on, Leonard Cohen. Happy birthday, and many more. Eighty is but a stepping stone in your Tower of Song.

October 15, 2014

ALSO BY TOM TEICHOLZ

Greetings from Tommywood, Volume One.
Son of Tommywood, Volume Two.
Tommywood III: The Column Strikes Back
Fast Furious Tommywood, Volume Five.
Close Encounters of the Tommywood Kind, Volume Six.
Wilshire Boulevard Temple and the Warner Murals: Celebrating 150 Years by Tom Teicholz, Oro Editions, San Francisco, CA 2014.
The Trial of Ivan The Terrible: State of Israel vs. John Demjanjuk by Tom Teicholz, St.Martin's Press, New York, New York, 1990.
Like No Other Store: Bloomingdale's and the Revolution in American Marketing by Marvin Traub and Tom Teicholz, Times Books/Random House, New York, New York, 1993.
Conversations with Jerzy Kosinski, edited and with an introduction by Tom Teicholz, University Press of Mississippi, Jackson, Mississippi.
Conversations with S. J. Perelman, edited and with an introduction by Tom Teicholz, University Press of Mississippi, Jackson, Mississippi.
The Jewish Role in American Life, Casden Insitute Annual Study, Volume 1, by Barry Glassner, Hillary Lachner, and Tom Teicholz, USC / Casden Institute, Los Angeles, CA.

Other books and anthologies containing Tom Teicholz's work:

Conversations with Isaac Bashevis Singer, University Press of Mississippi, Jackson, Mississippi.
Writers at Work, Volume 8, The Paris Review Interviews, Viking/Penguin, New York.
Encyclopedia Judaica, Second Edition. Tom Teicholz, American Film and TV editor.

ACKNOWLEDGMENTS

I am grateful to *The Jewish Journal* where this work originally appeared in print; and to the editors, proofreaders, and designers who made my work more readable; and to The Huffington Post for allowing me to repost my work there.

I also want to thank the contributors to The TOMMYWOOD Collection IndieGogo campaign for their support and generosity which made publication possible, most notably my tzadiks, hoochems and benefactors: Sandy Climan, Bracken Darrell, Lawrence Schoen, Toni and John Schulman, Bob & Cori Davenport, Peter Graham and Heidi Drymer, Ken & Teri Hertz, Wally & Helen Weiss, Dede Arnholz, Chuck Leavitt, Sharon Nazarian, Chris Pilkington, Stacy and Massimo Pinello, Robert & Edie Parker, Annie Scichili, and Richard Wolloch.

There is more to a book than just writing its content. You need talented people to successfully prepare it for publication. The reason this book looks so terrific is because of designer Devin Tanchum and the very talented folks at Rare Bird Lit, notably my book guru Tyson Cornell and his excellent associates Alice Elmer and Violet Sarosi, as well as Winona Leon (who did the design work for my IndieGogo Campaign). I also want to thank John Vaskis and John Trigonis at IndieGogo for teaching me so much about crowdfunding and helping make this book possible.

ABOUT THE AUTHOR

Tom Teicholz is an award-winning journalist, producer, and content consultant who has created print, video, and social media content for Intel, The Museum of Tolerance, The Milken Family Foundation, as well as for several not-for-profits and private clients. His work has appeared in *The New York Times Sunday Magazine*, *The Los Angeles Times Op-Ed* page, *Newsweek*, *The Paris Review*, *The New Yorker*'s 'Talk of the Town', *Narrative Magazine*, and *The Huffington Post*. He lives with his wife and daughter in Santa Monica, CA.

www.ingramcontent.com/pod-product-compliance
Lightning Source LLC
Chambersburg PA
CBHW032037290426
44110CB00012B/836